COSMOS OF THE ANCIENTS

Mourning Athena. Marble relief, c. 470 BC.

COSMOS OF THE ANCIENTS

THE GREEK PHILOSOPHERS ON MYTH AND COSMOLOGY

STEFAN STENUDD

arriba.se

Stefan Stenudd is a Swedish author, historian of ideas, artist, and a long-time instructor in the peaceful martial art aikido. He has published a number of books in Sweden as well as English, both fiction and non-fiction.

Among the latter is an interpretation of the Chinese classic *Tao Te Ching* and one of the Japanese samurai classic *Go Rin no Sho* by Miyamoto Musashi. His novels explore existential subjects from Stone Age drama to science fiction, but lately stay more and more focused on the present. He has also written some plays for the stage and the screen. In the history of ideas he studies the thought patterns of creation myths, as well as Aristotle's *Poetics*. He has his own extensive website:
www.stenudd.com

Also by Stefan Stenudd:
Tao Te Ching. The Taoism of Lao Tzu Explained, 2011.
Life Energy Encyclopedia, 2009.
Aikido Principles, 2008.
Qi. Increase Your Life Energy, 2008.
Attacks in Aikido, 2008.
Aikibatto. Sword Exercises for Aikido Students, 2007.
Your Health in Your Horoscope. Introduction to Medical Astrology, 2009.

Fiction:
All's End, 2007.
Murder, 2006.

Cover: Antisthenes. Roman copy of a Greek marble original from around 300 BC. *Frontispiece*: Parthenon, the temple of Athena on Acropolis in Athens, from the 5th century BC.

Stefan Stenudd: Cosmos of the Ancients. The Greek Philosophers on Myth and Cosmology
Copyright © Stefan Stenudd, 2007, 2011.
Cover and book design by the author.
All rights reserved.
ISBN 978-91-7894-045-5
Publisher: Arriba, Malmö, Sweden, info@arriba.se, www.arriba.se

CONTENTS

FOREWORD

Although this book is about philosophers, its objective is not philosophy. I am mainly interested in the patterns of thought, as they appear in religion and its myths. So, I use the Greek philosophers to explore how the human mind relates to religious beliefs: does it really believe in them?

Modern society is quite secular, and many among us have little faith in whatever religion our society supports. Still, we take for granted that in past cultures the population was homogenous in a strong belief in their gods and the myths about them. We tend to make the same assumption about any society outside of our own, and any religion except the one of our own tradition.

That is hasty, probably also prejudiced. Why would we not start by expecting other cultures to be able the same doubts?

The Greek philosophers lived in a society that cherished the myths about its gods, celebrated them and erected temples to their honor. It is taken for granted that the Greeks of Antiquity believed in their gods and the myths about them, as if their minds were unable of anything else. Now, the minds of the philosophers are accessible to us in the form of their words saved for posterity. Their thoughts can be traced, as for how they related to the gods worshiped by the society surrounding them.

Those were excellent minds, of course. Maybe they had little in common with the thoughts going through the heads of the average citizens at that time. Still, there is a limit to how much different they could have been. What was conceivable to the philosophers must at least have been perceivable to other Greeks. Otherwise their words would neither have been understood nor recorded. And they were no alien beings.

So, what the Greek philosophers were thinking, was possible for anyone in their society to think. If they doubted the existence of the gods or the accuracy of the myths, then that doubt was recognizable to other Greeks, and quite possibly present in their minds as well.

As can be seen in this book, the doubt was definitely there – just about everywhere.

That is reason enough to start by assuming the same doubt in every culture and every era. We have our religions, our gods and myths. Even though we may cherish and praise them, we also have our doubts about them. I would say that it's not a question of whether the human mind is capable of doubt – the question is really if we are at all able not to doubt. I doubt it.

Stefan Stenudd
April, 2007

INTRODUCTION

LIVING MYTH

It is a rare thing being able to study a setting of living myth, with numerous contemporary commentators to it, people writing in that setting at the very time of the myth's flourishing. Thereby, several important questions can be answered, such as: What roles do the myths play in their life? Do they regard the myths as perfectly accurate recounts of past events? Do they see the myths as trustworthy guides in the present? How do they interpret and understand them?

Of course, this study can be done – at least orally – in a number of societies around the world where the myths are still integrated with social life and not marginalized or defeated by cosmologies of other kinds. On the other hand, in such societies – for example, the many remaining hunter-gatherer cultures – the local commentators are extremely difficult for the outside observer to understand with any certainty. It is also possible that their language contains few terms for analyzing their traditions in any alternative way.

Language and thought are bound to the framework of the society they belong to. This is particularly true about cultures without writing, which is the tool for analytical discussion continued through time. Oral tradition can keep impressive amounts of information relatively intact for generations, but with little abstraction or theoretical reasoning.[1] Stories are easily kept and repeated, but not speculations about them.

Even if their language and minds are apt to it, what's to guarantee that it's not lost in translation? It has proven difficult enough for outside observers to digest local myths and cosmologies. To follow local discussions on their objective value and accuracy, if such conversations are at all possible, would be quite complex.

Already to find a trustworthy local source is no easy matter. The brothers Villas Boas spent as much as 25 years with the Xingu Indians in Brazil. Still, they confessed to this problem:

> *One of the most difficult things in obtaining this kind of data is to find the best informant. An Indian who speaks our language well and who readily offers to tell us stories or reveal information is precisely the least trustworthy for this purpose. True informants never come forward on their own, they speak only their own language, and when they are questioned, they even draw back. Furthermore, there are never more than one or two true trustees of the spiritual culture in each village.*[2]

Even if the people in question is as willing as ever to share its thoughts, and the listener is all ears, problems

[1] About the nature of oral contrary to written tradition, see Ong, Walter J., *Orality and Literacy. Technologizing of the Word*, London 1982.

[2] Villas Boas, Orlando & Claudio, *Xingu: the Indians, their Myths*, translated by Susana Hertelendy Rudge, London 1974, p.49f.

appear. French anthropologist Marcel Griaule was by the tribe elders allowed an introduction to the Dogon people's cosmology. His teacher was Ogotemmêli, one of the elders, who estimated that it would take years to complete the teaching. On one of those lectures, Griaule reacted to an inconsistency in the cosmological structure described. Ogotemmêli had told him about a small celestial surface, which had more animals than there could possibly be room for. Ogotemmêli was quick to reply:

> *"All this had to be said in words," said Ogotemmêli, "but everything on the steps is a symbol, symbolic antelopes, symbolic vultures, symbolic hyenas." He paused for a moment, and added: "Any number of symbols could find room on a one-cubit step."*
>
> *For the word 'symbol' he used a composite expression, the literal meaning of which is 'word of this (lower) world'.*[3]

About the multifaceted problem of interpretation, the influential Historian of Religion Mircea Eliade wrote:

> *When, in one or two generations, perhaps even earlier, we have historians of religions who are descended from Australian, African or Melanesian tribal societies, I do not doubt that, among other things, they will reproach*

---

[3] Griaule, Marcel, *Conversations with Ogotemmêli: an Introduction to Dogon Religious Ideas* (*Dieu d'eau: entretiens avec Ogotemmêli*, 1948), London 1965, p.37.

Western scholars for their indifference to the scale of values indigenous to these societies.[4]

That, we are still waiting for. Furthermore, it's no guarantee. The prominent anthropologist E. E. Evans-Pritchard was even more pessimistic about our ability to correctly perceive the belief systems of those cultures:

Statements about a people's religious beliefs must always be treated with the greatest caution, for we are then dealing with what neither European nor native can directly observe, with conceptions, images, words, which require for understanding a thorough knowledge of a people's language and also an awareness of the entire system of ideas of which any particular belief is part".[5]

In the same paragraph he warns: "speaking a language fluently is very different from understanding it".

REALITY

We must remind ourselves that the idea of reality as something separate from myth is not necessarily shared by other cultures – actually not even by our own, as it was just centuries ago, or for that matter still might be in certain aspects that we do not ourselves notice.

[4] Eliade, Mircea, *The Quest: History and Meaning in Religion*, Chicago 1969, p.75.

[5] Evans-Pritchard, E. E., *Theories of Primitive Religion*, Oxford 1965, p.7.

Basically, it's all in the mind. What we perceive and how we relate to it comes first for every person in any culture. Objective facts, separate from our perception, are relevant to us only if we have some use for them or need to relate to them in some way. Therefore, we all tend to regard as real that which fits our needs the best.

Myths always speak of past events, particularly so creation myths. Since the past is no longer present, it tends to be regarded in a way that is the most appreciated at the time. Our modern society is no exception. We analyze myth as well as history with the tools of our own time.

The whole notion of objective fact as something contrary to and separable from the imaginary, and putting great value on a distinction between the two, is a western thing. It has not even been consistently observed through our history. We cannot assume that this has been done as vigorously in other societies, as it has in ours for the last hundred years or so.

When examining the myths of a culture very different from our own, we should also try to grasp its attitudes to reality as opposed to imagination, fact as opposed to fiction, their use and interpretation of symbols, and so forth.

Not an easy task, but nonetheless essential if we are to get some kind of understanding of the role of myth in other cultures. Maybe we have little hope of perceiving any more than what those alien myths seem to mean to us. Maybe myth is impenetrable to someone outside of the society in which it is kept, and within that society it is impossible to distance oneself from its myths. Either the forest or the trees – never both.

It would be much easier to approach people's intellectual relations to their myths closer to home, so to speak. And this can be done – with the Greeks of ancient times.

Achilles with a Gorgon headed shield. Terracotta relief from about 600 BC. The Gorgons were female monsters. A man turned into stone by looking at a Gorgon's face.

THE GREEKS

The ideas of western society are to a large extent formed in antique Greece by its philosophers, who lived in a time when the Greek myths were very much alive. Much of their thoughts and discussions remains in written form, in a language and a way of reasoning that we are accustomed to, through over 2000 years. It still needs some deciphering, and our interpretations of their thoughts are still to some extent uncertain, but there is no source of thought from another culture that we can hope to do better with.

So, how did the Greeks relate to the myths and to the cosmology those myths presented?

Paul Veyne, professor of Roman history at the Collège de France in Paris, dedicated a book to the subject: *Did the Greeks Believe in their Myths?*[6] His approach is the question of truth and untruth, belief and disbelief, in a broader sense, and not isolating it to the Greeks. He makes a distinction between believing in a myth or other story on one hand, and believing in the elements of the myth having an objective existence outside of the story on the other:

> *These legendary worlds were accepted as true in the sense that they were not doubted, but they were not accepted the way that everyday reality is.*[7]

[6] Veyne, Paul, *Did the Greeks Believe in their Myths? An Essay on the Constitutive Imagination,* translated by Paula Wissing, Chicago 1988 (the French original was published in 1983).

[7] Veyne, p.17.

He compares it to the common relation of any reader to a work of fiction: people believe in *Madame Bovary* while they read it.[8]

While reading, we believe that what we read is true. Only afterward do we call it fiction.[9]

This is the 'contract' between an audience and any form of story-telling, well known also in the theater and the movies. He refers to what he calls the constitutive imagination, pointing out that "each epoch thinks and acts within arbitrary and inert frameworks."[10] Our impression of reality is bound by our culture and other surrounding circumstances. To Veyne, truth is nothing more than an impression of the imagination: "Men do not find the truth: they create it, as they create their history."[11] Thereby he seems to conclude that the question of the book's title is irrelevant.

In his investigation of the matter he focuses primarily, almost exclusively, on the writing of Pausanias (flourished c.160 CE) and his *Description of Greece*, a book reporting extensively about all kinds of Greek myth.

Veyne's view is easy enough to agree with. It is not the least controversial. Certainly, a myth – any story – has its inner cosmology, which needs to be accepted as long as we are inside this story, listening to it, reading it, seeing it per-

[8] Veyne, p.117.

[9] Veyne, p.103.

[10] Veyne, p.118.

[11] Veyne, p.xii.

formed. For me, though, it is of greater interest what people may have thought about those stories at the end of their telling or performing. Were the myths regarded as true outside of their own realm? This, Veyne does not investigate.

The myths in question, mainly those of Homer and Hesiod, were well established in society and integrated in its cultural life, in the days of the philosophers. The gods were worshiped – feared, too – and the myths about them were not told as fairytales to children, but as actual events having taken place in this world long ago. They were credited with authenticity and significance.

The Greek philosophers may have had little in common with ordinary citizens of Athens, but they do bear witness to some human relations to the myths, their gods and cosmology, at the time when these were integrated with social life. Even if their thoughts were shared by few outside their group – which seems not to have been the case – they did live in that society. What they were able to discuss was indeed possible for members of that society to discuss. They show what thoughts on the myths were possible, and what theories about the world were conceivable.

Of particular interest for this text are their views on mythological narrative of how the world came to be, and what powers may rule its continued existence – the cosmogony and cosmology of it all. I allow more room for their thoughts than their actual mythological theories may call for, and I sketch their cosmological views, whether they contain gods and myths or not. Their discussions reveal what intellectual framework existed at their time, be it only for the most learned, and what it may tell about their beliefs. In that way, their dependence or independence of the myths is visible.

It also gives a good example of human reasoning about such great things as the very birth and inner workings of the world, without having all the facts. The Greek philosophers had a minimum of scientific facts for support, little more than what was visible around them, when pondering cosmological matters. Their way of using – or ignoring – this limited material shows quite clearly how they thought and progressed toward their cosmology.

GOD

The word *god* is vastly used but rarely defined. In the modern western world its meaning is greatly influenced by the Judeo-Christian god of the Bible, and the traditions of those two religions. This image of god has to be forgotten, when considering the Greeks and their gods.

The Greek word translated to god is *theos*, which is masculine, and the feminine *thea*. The plural form is *theoi*, particularly relevant to Greek mythology, where there is a multitude of gods. The word's etymology is not clear, but possibly its Indo-European roots are connected to concepts of something holy and festive. This implies ritual and devotion. Alternatively the term might stem from words meaning smoke or spirit.

To the Greeks of Antiquity *theoi* referred to the immortals portrayed by Homer and Hesiod, but the word was also used by the philosophers in their speculations about higher powers, as presented in this book. For the purpose of this book, we need not expand the definition and analysis of the word *god* any further than those two Greek uses of it.

SELECTION

In the following, I present 27 Greek philosophers from Thales to Euhemerus. This is hardly a complete listing, although regarding the pre-Socratics not far from it. These philosophers are chosen mainly because they are mentioned in literature on mythology and religion, as having in some way discussed it. Some of them, like Euhemerus and Theagenes, always pop up in historical introductions to the theory of myth and religion, whereas others included here are almost never mentioned, but I find their views valuable in this context.

In many books on the subject of the Greek philosophers' views on myth, there is an unquestioning transport of the names frequently mentioned, so that they appear in most texts but are analyzed in very few of them. Standard statements about them, not always accurate, are simply passed on. That goes for the two mentioned above, as well as for Protagoras, Antisthenes and others. To avoid this, I have tried as much as possible to examine the fragments remaining of their own words, and looked at their cosmological views in general, to find how they might fit with what we believe about their relation to the myths and the gods.

For the same reason, that of not just repeating the conventional reports, I have not grouped them according to periods, schools, or any other system introduced after their own days. Below, the order is that of their date of flourishing, as well as it can be established. Flourishing, *acme*, is traditionally used mainly in dating the pre-Socratic philosophers, and equals their fortieth year of living.

Several of the philosophers appear to have similar, if not sometimes identical views on the matters in focus here. Their cosmological speculations are similar, they express similar doubts as to what can be stated about reality, or what can or cannot be said about the gods. Grouping them in categories would not be difficult, at least not with the majority of them. Still, I have tried my best to present each individual philosopher's cosmology as I have perceived it, not molding him to fit a certain category.

SOURCES

It must be remembered that very little remains of the writing of most Greek philosophers, especially those before Plato. Their words have reached us in fragments – quotes in other writings, mostly of much later dates. These later writers, though, probably had access to the books in question, or in some cases other texts quoting them in a trustworthy way.

The dominant source on pre-Socratic philosophers is Diogenes Laertius, who presented and quoted them substantially in *Lives of Eminent Philosophers*, probably written in the 3rd century CE. He was himself an Epicurean philosopher, but not much more is known about him. He obviously had an impressive library at hand. All in all, he makes 1,186 explicit references to 365 books by about 250 authors, almost all of them lost to us. Also, there are more than 350 anonymous references.[12] Mainly these are secondary or tertiary sources. He did not have many of the books by the philosophers themselves, although he lists a multitude of such titles.[13]

There have been differing opinions about how trustworthy his book is, but it is clear that he took it upon himself to do as good a job with it as he could, showing an impressive care about detail and keeping a critical mind.

He frequently questioned his own sources where they were doubtful, and often gave several versions where he had found them in his library. The book is not propagating his own philosophy, although it occasionally taints his explanations. As a whole, he gives a strong impression of trying to present the philosophers justly, for their own sake. The very title of his book shows his respect for them.

Among the few sources contemporary to the philosophers is Aristotle, who presents and discusses several of the philosophers in his writing. So does Plato, although to a lesser extent. Most other sources are of later dates, and usually contain only a brief mention and short quotes.

So, the treasure of Greek philosophy has been reconstructed from bits and pieces, with the exception of Plato and Aristotle, who have reached us with an abundance of writing, drowning their colleagues. Of course, this makes for an odd balance in our perception of Greek philosophy, especially since the two had the relation of teacher and pupil,

---

[12] Diogenes Laertius, *Lives of Eminent Philosophers*, translated by R. D. Hicks, volume I, Loeb, London 1995, p.xix.

[13] Diogenes Laertius, volume I, p.xxiv.

although differing considerably in their thinking and writing. In this book, I have made an effort to even the score by presenting also the views of the other philosophers, even when very little of their thinking remains.

The scarcity of sources opens for doubts about several of the facts given about the philosophers. For example, it is striking how old almost all of them seem to have gotten. The dates of their births and deaths that we have, show a number of philosophers reaching and passing their 80's. Pythagoras reached 82, Xenophanes 92, Gorgias 105, Democritus 103 according to some and about 90 according to others, Antisthenes and Plato 80, and a number of the others got into their 70's.

Certainly, life in Athens was agreeable to many of its citizens in those days, if they could avoid war and refrain from provoking the authorities. Yet, these long lives should be regarded with some scepticism. The life-expectancy for children born today in Greece is 79 years, but in Classical Greece the average life span was no more than about 25 years – mainly due to high infant mortality. In Classical Rome, a child reaching 10 years would have a life-expectancy of 50, but only 2% of the population reached the age of 70.[14] The figures for Classical Greece are unlikely to differ significantly from those of Rome.

Philosophers of dignity were supposed to reach old age, so their dates may have been adjusted accordingly. It is also

---

[14] These figures concern Classical Rome, but should be very similar for Classical Greece. Riggsby, Andrew M., *Roman Life Expectancy*, utexas.edu/depts/classics/documents/Life.html

possible that they had to get old to be respected and established enough for posterity to remember them. Still, there is reason for questioning the birth and death years given about several of the philosophers.

Regarding many of the pre-Socratic philosophers, there is little consensus about the years of their birth and death in today's literature. The dates given can differ as much as decades between one source and the other, for example with Philolaus, Melissus, or Heraclitus, but mostly the difference is just a couple of years. Still, this is quite annoying, considering that the Greek philosophers have been studied with devotion for so long, in so many countries and cultures. The years I give are sort of means, from comparing the sources I have used for this book, and in some cases I have chosen the date supported by the strongest argument.

Also the information about teacher and pupil seems to be doubtful. In some cases, the age difference between those said to be pupils and their teacher is either too big or too small. Pythagoras was two years older than Pherecydes and still supposed to be his pupil. Between Parmenides and (according to some sources) his teacher Xenophanes the difference was as much as 55 years, between Anaxagoras and his reported teacher Anaximenes 85 years, between Empedocles and Pythagoras as much as 92, and between Empedocles and Gorgias only seven years, while Protagoras is said to have been the pupil of Democritus although he was 21 years his senior. It is likely that some have been linked as teacher and pupil simply because of similarities in their theories.

Fortunately, questions of their lifespan or teachers are of little importance here. Still, these discrepancies should be taken as warnings of how fragile our knowledge is of the Greek philosophers.

In spelling the names, I follow the Latin form in accordance with most of the literature on Greek philosophy in the English language. In quotes and references, though, I follow the spelling of the source in question.

There is an increasing tendency also in English literature to use a spelling closer to the original Greek pronunciation of the names. Therefore, I have added these spellings, within parenthesis, when presenting each thinker.

LAW

Doubting the cosmology and gods of Greek society was not only a question of reason or ethics. It was also a matter of the law. Before examining what Greek thinkers had to say about the gods, it must be considered what they were allowed to say.

Through the history of Christianity, the risk of offending the Church and the Law silenced many tongues and made writers choose their words very carefully, indeed. Ancient Greek society had similar restrictions, but it seems that those were neither as sharp in letter or as stern in prosecution, as Christianity would later make them. With the decrease of the number of gods there was an equally drastic increase in impiety regulation and punishment.

Old Greece had laws regarding the gods and "the things of the gods", but there was no religious institution handling such matters. They were decided and dealt with in the same way as any other matter in society, by the same civil bodies.[15] These rules dealt primarily with rituals and behavior connected to them, such as "wrongdoings concerning a festival", "theft of sacred money" and "temple robbing", the last of which was regarded the most seriously.[16]

There were few crimes normally leading to the death penalty. Blasphemous speech was rarely one of them. Xenophon quotes Socrates saying:

> *Since not even my accusers themselves allege against me that I have committed any of those deeds of which death is the penalty, such as robbery of temples, breaking into houses, selling freemen into slavery, or betrayal of the state; so that I must still ask myself in wonderment how it has been proved to you that I have done a deed worthy of death.*[17]

Impiety could also be a punishable crime, but there seems to have been no clear definition of it. In the known cases, the accusations concerned introducing new gods, other than the ones of the tradition. Alternative explanations to cosmology and natural phenomena could be regarded as introducing new gods. That would have made almost every

---

[15] Parker, Robert, Law and Religion, in Gagarin and Cohen (ed.), *The Cambridge Companion to Ancient Greek Law*, Cambridge 2005, p.61.

[16] Parker, p.63f.

[17] Xenophon, *The Apology*, translated by Henry Graham Dakyns, Gutenberg.

Greek philosopher a criminal, but only a few were accused of such a crime. Socrates was executed in 399 BC for it. The formal indictment was:

> *Socrates does wrong by not acknowledging the gods the city acknowledges, and introducing other, new powers. He also does wrong by corrupting the young.*[18]

About other thinkers having been prosecuted for similar reasons – such as Anaxagoras, Protagoras, and Prodicus – the circumstances are uncertain. The sources are of later dates, and often clearly untrustworthy. Where there were such trials leading to severe punishment, additional charges or circumstances were involved.[19]

Socrates. Greek statuette from about the 2nd century BC.

In the case of Socrates, Plato lets us know in *Apology* that he provoked the jury of 501 citizens by suggesting a punishment for his crime that would actually be a reward. The only alternative the jurors had was the death penalty, so that was what they voted for – with a greater majority than the one by which he had been declared guilty.

[18] Parker, p.67.

[19] Parker, p.66f.

Xenophon suggests that Socrates sought to receive the death-penalty, since he was quite old and found it an easier way out than the prolonged decay of age:

> Socrates did, it is true, by his self-laudation draw down upon him the jealousy of the court and caused his judges all the more to record their votes against him. Yet even so I look upon the lot of destiny which he obtained as providential, chancing as he did upon the easiest amidst the many shapes of death, and escaping as he did the one grievous portion of existence.[20]

Both Plato and Xenophon were convinced that Socrates could have escaped the death-penalty, maybe even a conviction, if he had wanted to.

Clearly, doubting the gods publicly could be unsafe, but normally far from as devastating as it would get to be when Christianity ruled. The Greek philosophers as well as other citizens could voice a disbelief in the gods, as long as they were polite about it.

[20] Xenophon, *The Apology*.

Theseus carries off Helen. Later, Paris of Troy will do the same to her, which leads to the Trojan war. Vase painting.

HOMER AND HESIOD

Greek literature began in the Mycenaean period (circa 1600-1100 BC) as stories told aloud. The Mycenaeans had a pictorial script (*Linear B*), but used it for accounting and records of stock – a use that was also the first for the Sumerian writing, the oldest one known. Wars between 1200 to 1000 BC weakened Greek knowledge of writing, until they adopted an alphabet from Phoenicia in the 8th century BC. The works of Homer and Hesiod are the oldest texts written with that alphabet.

When the ancient day Greeks discussed matters of gods and their doings, the sources they almost exclusively referred to were Homer and Hesiod. Their texts were regarded as such outstanding sources, as if Homer and Hesiod had been the discoverers, if not inventors, of the gods.

Herodotus, the historian of the 5th century BC, made the influence of Homer and Hesiod quite clear:

It was these who constructed a divine genealogy for the Greeks and who gave the gods their titles, allocated their powers and privileges to them, and indicated their forms.[21]

As far back as we have traces of a discussion about their writings, they have been regarded ambiguously, to say the least. The adventurous gods portrayed in the *Iliad* and the *Odyssey*, as well as those majestic beings roaming in the

---

[21] Hesiod, *Theogony and Works and Days*, translated by M. L. West, Oxford 1988, p.xx.

Theogony, are often beastly, monstrous. The way they allow their emotions to rule their actions – more often than not resulting in mayhem – is nothing commendable in the mind of most Greek philosophers. The texts on the individual philosophers below give several examples of this.

Homer

Homer (Homeros) may have lived in the 8th century BC. Almost nothing is certain about him – for example if he existed at all, a question that has been heavily debated among the experts. If there was no Homer, the *Iliad* and *Odyssey* were collected through an oral tradition. This is supported by elements of their form.[22]

Homer. Roman marble copy of a Greek bust from c. 460 BC.

They were put to writing no later than in the 6th century BC, but there is no evidence to suggest a fixed date of their initial making. Recently, an estimate has been made by Richard Janko, through linguistic analysis of the poems.[23] He concludes that the *Iliad* was composed around 750-725 BC, and the *Odyssey* 743-713, but his result is far from certain.

Homer's texts present the gods as active participants in the adventures described. Several Greek thinkers have criticized him for portraying the gods in far from flattering ways. He shows them having quite human traits – noble as well as low ones. They fight alongside or against human beings,

---

[22] About the elements revealing an oral origin, see Ong, Walter J., *Orality and Literacy. Technologizing of the Word*, London 1982.

[23] Janko, Richard, *Homer, Hesiod and the Hymns: Diachronic Development in Epic Diction*, Cambridge 1982, p.xvi and 322.

rarely with any higher goals. They also fight repeatedly against each other.

Divine interference with human affairs is evident from the very start of the *Iliad*:

> *Sing, goddess, the wrath of Achilles Peleus' son, the ruinous wrath that brought on the Achaians woes innumerable, and hurled down into Hades many strong souls of heroes, and gave their bodies to be a prey to dogs and all winged fowls; and so the counsel of Zeus wrought out its accomplishment from the day when first strife parted Atreides king of men and noble Achilles.*
>
> *Who among the gods set the twain at strife and variance? Apollo, the son of Leto and of Zeus; for he in anger at the king sent a sore plague upon the host, so that the folk began to perish, because Atreides had done dishonour to Chryses the priest.*[24]

---

[24] Homer, *The Iliad*, translation by W. Leaf, 1891, gutenberg.org/etext/ 3059.

Hesiod

Hesiod (Hesiodos) probably lived in the 8th century BC, maybe close to 700 BC. His actual existence is not certain, but less debated than that of Homer, mainly because his texts contain some biographical information about himself. He wrote *Theogony* and *Works and Days*, which are regarded to have reached their final forms at the end of the 8th century or early 7th century BC.

Possibly Hesiod. Formerly believed to be Seneca. Roman copy of a Greek 2nd Century BC original.

It is the *Theogony* that contains Hesiod's cosmology, from the moment of the world's creation. It is filled with gods and divine spectacles:

> *First came the Chasm;[25] and then broad-breasted Earth,*
> *secure seat for ever of all the immortals who occupy the*
> *peak of snowy Olympus; the misty Tartara[26] in a remote*
> *recess of the broad-pathed earth; and Eros, the most*
> *handsome among the immortal gods, dissolver of flesh,*
> *who overcomes the reason and purpose in the breasts of*
> *all gods and all men.*

[25] Chasm is the literal meaning of the Greek word Chaos, without the present meaning of disorder or confusion. Hesiod, *Theogony*, translated by M. L. West, Oxford's World Classics, Oxford 1988, p.64.

[26] Dark and dreadful regions below Earth. Mostly spoken of in singular: Tartarus.

Out of the Chasm came Erebos[27] and dark Night,
and from Night in turn came Bright Air and Day, whom
she bore in shared intimacy with Erebos. Earth bore first
of all one equal to herself, starry Heaven,[28] so that he
should cover her all about, to be a secure seat for ever for
the blessed gods; and she bore the long Mountains,
pleasant haunts of the goddesses, the nymphs who dwell
in mountain glens; and she bore also the undraining Sea
and its furious swell, not in union of love. But then,
bedded with Heaven, she bore deep-swirling Oceanus[29],
Koios and Kreios and Hyperion and Iapetos, Thea and
Rhea and Themis and Memory, Phoebe of gold diadem,
and lovely Thetis. After them, the youngest was born,
crooked-schemer Kronos, most fearsome of children, who
loathed his lusty father.[30]

Hesiod goes on to tell the terrible tale of how the gods came into being, and how they fought their ancestors and each other, leading to Zeus becoming their victorious ruler. As M. L. West describes it:

It is a story of crude and bizarre acts of violence, of gods
castrating, swallowing, and generally clobbering each

---

[27] The realm of darkness, connected to Hades and Tartarus.

[28] Earth and Heaven are the gods Gaia and Ouranos (Uranus).

[29] A great river encircling the Earth.

[30] Hesiod, *Theogony*, translated by M. L. West, Oxford's World Classics, Oxford 1988, p.6f.

other in a way that sophisticated readers of Plato's time found strange and unacceptable.[31]

Hesiod's portrayal of the gods was criticized by several Greek thinkers, for the same reason as with Homer. Neither Hesiod's nor Homer's depiction of the gods is very flattering.

There is today an increasing conviction among scholars that the mythology of Hesiod is influenced substantially by Babylonian myths, such as the ones contained in *Enuma Elish* of the 11th century BC.[32] There, too, the gods fight brutally among themselves over rulership.

Hesiod presents about 300 gods in his *Theogony*, some well known and some peripheral or completely unheard of elsewhere. It is not unlikely that he invented a few gods, to make his genealogy and cosmology work out. He connected natural forces to divinities, such as Earth, Heaven, Sun and Moon. Also, he had abstract concepts represented by gods: Death, Sleep, Deceit, Strife, and so on.

In *Work and Days* he reveals his way of thinking about divine entities, when reasoning about rumor as a power that never dies, once it is released: "She too is somehow a goddess."[33]

The works of Homer and Hesiod became the canon of Greek religion, but they were written with other intentions. Both writers allowed themselves some creative editing of the myths they treated, for the purpose of making their stories

[31] Hesiod, p.xi.

[32] Hesiod, p.xii.

[33] Hesiod, p.x-xi.

work. In the adventures designed by Homer, and the grand spectacles of Hesiod's writing, the gods were tools rather than rulers. The true rulers of those events were the ones writing them down.

Euripides. Marble statue.

DRAMA AND POETRY

Myth as storytelling, with magnificent characters and spectacular events, comes naturally to the dramatists and poets – in those days regarded as one and the same profession. They had little problem with the question if myths are to be believed or not. Whether true or false, myths make good material for drama and poetry. So, within the drama or the poem, they are true. Of course, inventors of stories have no problem jumping from fact to imagination and back again, not caring to make any distinction between them. That is their trade.

In Greece, drama had its golden age in the 5th century BC, while philosophy had its peak during the following century, with Plato and Aristotle. Those two philosophers confess to the influence the great dramas had on them – Aristotle with more delight than Plato. It must have been true for all the thinkers of the era. The mythical and the divine met the Athenians spectacularly through the arts, maybe more so than in ritual and worship, so it was bound to influence their perception of such matters, as well as their views on them.

The artistic treatment of myths and gods is difficult indeed to analyze in search of a cosmology, or of answers to the question if the myths were believed or not. Drama and poetry were no treatises of natural science. The real and the unreal were used for other purposes than a search for truth. Little more can be stated, than that the poets did not fear the gods that much, since they dared to use them in stories – and not always flattering.

It is also questionable that they felt any obligation to treat the myths and gods in accordance with tradition. They must have needed to conform to generally known components, not changing basic concepts of myths and gods, or their audience would react and be unable to follow the story. Other than that, they could treat the material as they pleased, and if the result was appealing to their audiences, they may even have succeeded in changing or adding to a myth, as well as in transforming the perception of a god slightly.

This possibility should be considered also with Homer and Hesiod. Even if there were myths and gods established by oral tradition before them, they may very well have changed things according to their own liking. In whatever way the *Iliad*, *Odyssey* and *Theogony* were written down, the myths are quite likely to have been reshaped in many ways during this process. It should not be assumed that they were regarded as fact, even by their oral transmitters or those who were the first to write them down.

The poets were clearly able to raise the question if the myths and the gods were to be believed or not. In *The Knights*, played and awarded first prize at the Lenaean festival in 424 BC, Aristophanes puts this doubt in the mouth of a slave, at the bottom of Athenian society. One unfortunate slave says to his comrade: "The only thing left to do is to throw ourselves at the feet of the gods," whereby the other slave responds: "Indeed! Say, then, do you really believe that there are gods?"[34]

---

[34] Veyne, Paul, *Did the Greeks Believe in their Myths? An Essay on the Constitutive Imagination*, translated by Paula Wissing, Chicago 1988, p.31f.

Since poetic treatment of the myths is so different from that of the philosophers, it must be considered separately. Below, the three poets most often mentioned in texts about myth are given as examples of poetic relation to myth and gods: Pindar, Euripides and Critias. What they actually thought about the matter can't be ascertained, but it is clear that they dared question the very existence of the gods.

Maybe poets are the most difficult to convince of anything at all, since they are by their own work familiar with how anything can be imagined. Still, there were poets expressing a firm support of the Greek multitude of gods, and doing it with a lyrical devotion approaching that of Homer and Hesiod.

Pindar

The lyrical poet Pindar (Pindaros, circa 520-476 BC), whose teacher was Apollodorus, would not have the gods treated disrespectfully. In the beginning of his *Olympian Odes* he states:

> *In truth it is seemly for man to say of the gods nothing ignoble; for so he giveth less cause for blame.*[35]

Pindar.

He goes on to tell how "some envious neighbors" have added to the story of the gods inviting a human being, Tanta-

---

[35] Sandys, John, *The Odes of Pindar*, Cambridge, Massachusetts 1946, p.7.

lus, to join them, that they cut him up and devoured him. "Far be it from me to call any one of the blessed gods a cannibal! I stand aloof."[36] He did not object to the idea of the gods acting mercilessly toward humans – but as punishment, well deserved, and not for some deranged pleasure of theirs.

To Pindar, the gods are distant and superior indeed. Mortal man cannot hope to find them. Because he is mortal, it is impossible for him. Yet, there is something in man, which does not suffer death, but is released from the body at the moment of its passing, and therefore has to be of divine origin:

> And, while the body of all men is subject to over-master-ing death, an image of life remaineth alive, for it alone cometh from the gods. But it sleepeth, while the limbs are active; yet, to them that sleep, in many a dream it giveth presage of a decision of things delightful or doleful.[37]

Pindar is one of the few Greeks who are clearly loyal to the gods of the myths – even more so than the myths them-selves are. As a poet, he allows himself an artistic perspective rather than a philosophical one. That may also have given him the incentive to scrutinize the stories about the gods,

---

[36] Sandys, p.9. Pindar's choice of word seems to imply anthropomorphy, if gods and men are so alike that it would be cannibalism, but I am not sure if the term actually used by Pindar implies anthropophagy, man eating man.

[37] Sandys, p.591.

accepting some and condemning others. He regards the gods as true, but not some demeaning stories about them.

It must be remembered that he wrote for festivals and rituals, wherefore his tone needed to be ceremonious, with a generous touch of the glorious. For that, he needed gods of grandeur.

The playwrights treated the gods with less awe, and examined the myths from other angles than that of the lyrical poet. Their art, dealing with the nature of man's mind, invited it. This was also the focus of their interest – the roles of gods and myths in the lives of men.

Euripides

Euripides (480-406 BC) allowed discussions on cosmology and such to enter his plays through the mouths of their characters. That does not guarantee their views to be identical with his own, but it gives an example of how these questions were discussed in his time, outside the philosophical schools.

He lets one of his characters reason in *Bacchae*:

> *The goddess Demeter, – she is earth, call her by whichever name you wish.*[38]

In the same monologue, the legend of Dionysos being sewn into the thigh of Zeus is explained as a change of word through time. Not that what Euripides regards as the authentic version is any less fabulous:

---

[38] Euripides, *Bacchae*, translated by Richard Seaford, Warminster 1996, p.83.

Having broken off a part of the air of heaven that encir-
cles the earth, he gave this as a hostage, removing Dio-
nysos from quarrels with Hera.[39]

Another reasoning, along the lines later repeated innu-
merable times in the Christian era and according to Euripides old already at his time, is the question how a benevolent
god could allow injustice. This is expressed in *Bellerophon*, a
drama remaining only in fragments:

Does someone say that there are gods in heaven?
There are not, there are not, if a man will
not in folly rely on the old argument.
Consider it yourselves; do not build your opinion
on my words. I say that a tyranny
kills many men and deprives them of their possessions,
and breaking oaths destroys cities;
and doing this they are more happy
than those who live each day in pious peace.
And I know of small cities that honor the gods
which obey greater and more impious ones,
overcome by the greater number of spears.[40]

[39] Euripides, *Bacchae*, p.83.

[40] Barnes, Jonathan, *The Presocratic Philosophers*, volume 2, London 1979,
p.152.

Critias

The Athenian statesman Critias (c. 455-403 BC) has given his name to one of Plato's dialogues, and participates also in *Timaeus* as one of Socrates' pupils. He was a poet and thinker of distinction in his days. He was also Plato's uncle. When Critias seized power and became one of the thirty tyrants, his rule was so terrible that he earned the title well. He died in battle, soon after that.

His view on the gods, bluntly expressed in his satyr-play *Sisyphus*, goes in line with the forceful leadership of his. Critias claimed that the gods had been consciously invented, to frighten the people into obedience and law-abiding life. Thus, the gods were all-seeing, so that no man should hope to conceal his crime, and their abode was heaven, the far-off place that induced the most fear in man with its thunder, lightning and celestial mysteries.

It is somewhat confusing that he put these words in the mouth of the Corinth king Sisyphus. According to legend, Sisyphus was punished by Zeus for telling on an amorous adventure of the god – in the torturous way of having to roll a stone up a steep hill, just to see it roll down again, and having to do it anew, without end. Sisyphus would regard the gods as very real, indeed.

The rest of the play is lost to us, so in what phase of the story this speech is delivered, we do not know. It would make sense to the drama if it occurs before Sisyphus meets with Zeus. If so, he could by this be meant to express a *hubris*, which needed punishment, with or without a disloyalty to Zeus adding to his crimes. It would imply a piety of

Critias, writing a moral play on hubris and its punishment, though that seems less in character with him than a flat agreement with what Sisyphus says.

Whatever the case, Sisyphus does in his monologue explain a process in society, a social cosmogony of sorts, which makes sense also to others than men of power:

There was a time when the life of men was unordered, bestial and the slave of force, when there was no reward for the virtuous and no punishment for the wicked. Then, I think, men devised retributory laws, in order that Justice might be dictator and have arrogance as its slave, and if anyone sinned, he was punished. Then, when the laws forbade them to commit open crimes of violence, and they began to do them in secret, a wise and clever man invented fear (of the gods) for mortals, that there might be some means of frightening the wicked, even if they do anything or say or think it in secret. Hence, he introduced the Divine, saying that there is a God flourishing with immortal life, hearing and seeing with his mind, and thinking of everything and caring about these things, and having divine nature, who will hear everything said among mortals, and will be able to see all that is done. And even if you plan anything evil in secret, you will not escape the gods in this; for they have surpassing intelligence. In saying these words, he introduced the pleasantest of teachings, covering up the truth with a false theory; and he said that the gods dwelt there where he could most frighten men by saying it, whence he knew

that fears exist for mortals and rewards for the hard life:
in the upper periphery, where they saw lightnings and
heard the dread rumblings of thunder, and the starry-
faced body of heaven, the beautiful embroidery of Time
the skilled craftsman, whence come forth the bright mass
of the sun, and the wet shower upon the earth. With such
fears did he surround mankind, through which he well
established the deity with his argument, and in a fitting
place, and quenched lawlessness among men ... Thus, I
think, for the first time did someone persuade mortals to
believe in a race of deities.[41]

This monologue is strikingly outspoken. Through the voice of Sisyphus, Critias expresses belief in no gods, no divine forces at all, just men and the deeds of men. To have been allowed such blasphemous utterances, be it through the character of a play, Critias must indeed have been a man of importance in Athens. Just about this time, Protagoras was driven out and his books burnt, merely for stating that the truth about the gods cannot be ascertained by man.

Critias went much further, claiming the gods not only to be invented by man, but also for such a worldly reason, where laws of men are given a higher priority than those of the divine. This was Heaven utilized for earthly ambitions. One marvels at the thought of his play actually having been performed afore the Athenians. That this man's cosmology must have been quite materialistic, is confirmed in another fragment of his:

---

[41] Freeman, Kathleen, *The Pre-Socratic Philosophers*, Oxford 1946, p.157f.

Nothing is certain, except that having been born we die,
and that in life one cannot avoid disaster.[42]

It is clear with both Euripides and Critias that they felt what we would call an artistic freedom toward the gods and the myths. This is no proof of either their belief or disbelief in them, but it reveals an ability in their minds to treat the tradition with some improvisations of their own, and to present the possibility of disbelief.

Of course, this also means that it was fathomable to their audiences. To playwright and audience alike, it was within reach of their minds both to have the myths altered, and to express a complete lack of faith in them. In drama, everything of gods and myths was possible to treat as products of the imagination.

[42] Freeman, p.160.

Deification of Homer. Homer is crowned at the bottom left, in front of actors. Above are the muses and several gods. Votive relief by Archelaos of Priene, 2ⁿᵈ century BC.

CATEGORIES OF COSMOLOGY

When sorting Greek theories on the divine and its mythology, I have allowed myself to use my own interpretation. This has sometimes been easy enough. In other cases it is the result of deduction with more or less solid support. Still, in the writings of the philosophers, there is good reason for the following categories.

First, a line is easily drawn between what can be called a *theistic* and an *atheistic* view. Philosophers belonging to the former standpoint express a belief in some kind of divine presence with a ruling influence over the world and what takes place on it, all the way back to its making. The latter group gives no role to gods in their cosmology, and expresses little faith in them, altogether.

A third group is needed, in between the two above mentioned – that of a cosmology neither including nor excluding gods, unquestionably. We can call the group *unclear*. Philosophers in this group do not support the gods of Homer and Hesiod, nor do they argue for any other divine force at work in the world – but they do not rule out the possibility.

Theistic

When using the term theistic as a way of grouping the philosophers, I consider to what extent they regard other than natural causes as instrumental in the workings of the world. God is a very vague concept, of course, but the idea of a superior will at work is found in the thoughts of many philosophers, even if they do not refer to the Greek gods in particular.

Several philosophers see just one such higher entity, in a kind of monotheistic cosmology. If their cosmos is instead populated by a number of divine beings, important entities separate from earthly life of living and dying, I categorize it as polytheistic.

Polytheistic is a cosmology including a number of gods – not necessarily those of Homer and Hesiod, but that is mostly the case. Therefore, this category is the closest to the cosmology of those two writers. Actually, it is only this kind of cosmology that agrees at all with Homer and Hesiod.

Although this is closest to the Greek myths, only one of the philosophers on my list belongs to the polytheistic category: Herodotus, who was actually a historian. Among the pure philosophers it is just not possible to find clear support for a polytheistic view. Also Herodotus is a questionable case. He does not state for certain that the gods exist as such, or ever did, but he does not rule it out.

Already by this, it is safe to say that the thinkers of old Greece were not at all bound by the myths, in their reflections on the world and its order. They allowed themselves to doubt, if not to refuse them completely. It must be assumed that they were not the only ones in Greek society capable of this perspective – or their words would not have been heard at all by their audiences.

Monotheistic signifies a view putting some kind of singular divine will at the top of it all, and accordingly lessening the importance of any other divinities, if not excluding them completely. The monotheistic perspective in Greek philosophy is more closely related to the atheistic than to the

polytheistic. This single divine force usually has the characteristics of natural law, more than of a divine being with
distinctive personality and sometimes questionable behavior.

Philosophers who believe in a multitude of gods are hard
to find in old Greece, but there is a number of thinkers who
imagine one divine being behind it all.

Whenever monotheism is reported in other cultures than
those encompassed by Christianity, we should be cautious
not to confuse it with either a later influence from Christianity or a distorted perspective by observers with a Christian
background. There is little risk of that in old Greece, though,
for obvious reasons of chronology, and because of lasting
documentation of the original Greek thoughts.

The idea of a high god, partly similar to that of the Bible,
is evident in the Greek tradition, represented by eight of the
philosophers on my list: Thales, Xenophanes, Heraclitus,
Anaxagoras, Antisthenes, Plato, Aristotle, and Zeno. Antisthenes, Plato and Aristotle were under Socratic influence, but
the others have no teacher to pupil relation.

Already at the beginning of Greek philosophy, with
Thales, the monotheistic perspective was present. Some of
these philosophers are not absolutely clear about whether
they allow for other lesser gods or not, but they all describe
a world ruled by one single deity. This leads to several other
similarities in their cosmology.

Unclear

Whatever category is applied to Greek thinkers, most of them fit less than perfectly in it. This is particularly true about such elusive concepts as gods and elements of cosmology.

In the theistic group above, several of the names can be discussed as to what extent they belong to it. That is also true for the atheistic group below. But this sorting is not essential to the treatment of the Greek philosophers in this book, so some discrepancies can be accepted. I have allowed myself to generalize and simplify when sorting them, since the tendencies are anyway obvious.

Those who express uncertainty about the gods as well as the myths about them, and those who treat them as allegories – without stating clearly if there is some divine reality to be found behind the allegories – need a group of their own.

The former view, which I call agnostic, is represented by just one philosopher: Protagoras. It seems that the Greek philosophers were not keen on voicing uncertainty.

The latter category, seeing the myths as allegory, contains five philosophers: Pherecydes, Pythagoras, Theagenes, Parmenides and Empedocles. Pherecydes and Pythagoras are said to have had a teacher to pupil relation, although the latter was slightly older of the two. The same is said about Pythagoras and Empedocles, although there are some 90 years between their time of flourishing.

One more group is needed, for those who have historical interpretations of the myths. They seek to explain the myths

as based on historical events, without any *deus ex machina*.[43]
No divine intervention, just people in worldly affairs, later
sort of spiced up by gods and heavenly effects.

So, the unclear perspective can be divided into three
categories: that of an agnostic cosmology, that of allegoric
interpretation of the myths, and that of an historical interpretation.

Agnostic I call the view which is uncertain, questioning
the existence of the gods, but not denying it. The agnostic
philosopher doubts the roles of gods in the making of the
world, but does not deem it impossible that divine beings are
at work. To this group belongs also the philosopher of the
traditional agnostic view that the truth of the matter is
impossible to ascertain.

The Greek philosophers were not eager to confess to
uncertainty about any issue, at least not according to the
texts by which they have reached us. In my list, there is only
one who claims that he does not know about divine matters:
Protagoras. But he also boldly states that it is impossible to
know.

Allegorical is the view which sees some more or less
divine doings behind the myths and the gods mentioned in
them, but not in the way they are recounted in those myths.
To those philosophers, natural forces as well as divine
principles are dressed in anthropomorphic costumes, but this

---

[43] *Deus ex machina*, god from a machine, is a Latin expression for when a
god appears and solves the situation in a drama. It is used about any
solution in a plot through the unexpected appearance of something or
someone not previously involved in the story. An easy way out for the
script writer. The original Greek expression is *theos apo mekhanes*.

does not necessarily mean that there are no divine beings at all.

Several Greek philosophers regarded the myths and their gods in an allegorical light, as symbolic representations of natural phenomena or principles by which the world works. It is not always clear whether the philosophers regarded the gods as pure inventions, without any kind of existence, or if they imagined true gods behind the allegorical representations. In any case, the philosophers who expressed an allegorical interpretation of myth have for that reason been put in this category.

Historical is the theory that the gods and myths about them have historical explanations, not divine at all. This is the principle of euhemerism, taking its name from Euhemerus, but he is not the only thinker with such a view. This cannot immediately be described as an atheistic perspective, if that is not outspoken. It does imply atheism, but since it is implied and not specified, this category must remain among the unclear.

The historical perspective on myths, claiming them to tell in a spectacular way of real events of the past, is represented by two Greek thinkers on my list. Both of them, Hecataeus and Euhemerus, should more rightly be called historians.

Especially with the latter, it can be questioned if he believed in anything divine at all. Still, I prefer to group him with the unclear instead of the atheists, since his theory still gives some credit to the myths and he has not stated in a definite way that there can be no gods of any kind. Hecataeus was ambiguous on this issue, but at the same time presenting himself as of divine ancestry.

Atheistic

Although they lived in a time where the gods were worshiped and the myths about them were very much alive in society, a substantial number of the Greek philosophers on my list had what can be described as an atheistic view. They did not believe in the gods of Homer and Hesiod, nor did they believe the world to be ruled by any divine beings.

The ten philosophers I put in this group are not all of them outspoken atheists. Some have what seems to be an agnostic or allegorical inkling, others may just be hesitant to express themselves categorically about this matter. Others yet see no necessity in either denying or accepting the existence of gods, because they find no role for them in their cosmology. In sorting them as atheists, I have merely examined their cosmology, and where it lacks a role for gods, there is no group they fit any better than this one.

Dividing the group into categories could be done on the characteristics of their cosmology. For example, some philosophers describe what could be called a mathematical universe, following strict logical laws, others see it as an arena of astronomical events, and so on. Such a division is of no use for the purpose of this book, though.

Of main interest is that they deny a divine ruler of the cosmos. Instead, they make elaborate explanations as to how the world could have appeared and continued, without some kind of god in control. They describe a world independent of gods, but nonetheless governed by universal principles. Doing so, the philosophers show themselves able of disregarding the gods and the myths altogether.

Categories
Here are the three categories of cosmology and their subdivisions, which I have used to sort the 27 philosophers treated in this book:

Categories of cosmology

Theistic	*Unclear*	*Atheistic*
Polytheistic	Agnostic	
Monotheistic	Allegorical	
	Historical	

GREEK PHILOSOPHERS CATEGORIZED
Here are two simple tables of the Greek philosophers treated in this book. The first table sorts them according to the category of their cosmology, the second by their year of flourishing. The second table also names their teacher.

In many cases the year of flourishing is rather uncertain. If very much so, I have noted it with a question mark. Sometimes there is also uncertainty as to whether they actually were pupils of the teacher mentioned, but when this is generally assumed I have just repeated the information. When there is good reason to doubt it, I have again used the question mark.

Finally, regarding the category in which I place their ideas on cosmology, this is of my own making, and not practiced in the history of philosophy. It is to show tendencies, only. What is said about each philosopher in the following chapters is of greater importance. Categories are rarely applicable to any other extent than as generalizations and approximations – especially in something as complex as human thinking.

The philosophers by category of cosmology

THEISTIC	UNCLEAR	ATHEISTIC
Polytheistic	*Agnostic*	Anaximander
Herodotus	Protagoras	Anaximenes
Monotheistic	*Allegorical*	Gorgias
Thales	Pherecydes	Melissus
Anaxagoras	Pythagoras	Leucippus
Heraclitus	Theagenes	Democritus
Antisthenes	Empedocles	Prodicus
Xenophanes	Parmenides	Diagoras
Plato	*Historical*	Epicurus
Aristotle	Hecataeus	Philolaus?
Zeno	Euhemerus	

The philosophers, their teacher and cosmology, chronologically

Flourished	Philosopher	Teacher	Cosmology
584 BC	Thales	Egyptians	monotheistic
570 BC	Anaximander	Thales?	atheistic
545 BC	Anaximenes	Anaximander	atheistic
542 BC	Pythagoras	Pherecydes?	allegorical
540 BC	Pherecydes of Syros	Pittacus	allegorical
530 BC	Xenophanes	none?	monotheistic
525 BC	Theagenes	?	allegorical
510 BC	Hecataeus	?	historical
502 BC	Heraclitus	none	monotheistic
475 BC	Parmenides	Xenophanes?	allegorical
460 BC	Anaxagoras	Anaximenes?	monotheistic
450 BC	Empedocles	Pythagoras?	allegorical
450 BC	Herodotus	?	polytheistic
443 BC	Gorgias	Empedocles	atheistic
442 BC	Melissus	Parmenides	atheistic
441 BC	Protagoras	Democritus?	agnostic
430 BC?	Philolaus	Pythagoras?	atheistic?
430 BC ?	Leucippus	Zeno	atheistic?
420 BC ?	Democritus	Leucippus	atheistic?
420 BC	Prodicus of Ceos	Protagoras	atheistic
406 BC	Antisthenes	Gorgias/Socrates	monotheistic
400 BC ?	Diagoras of Melos	Democritus	atheistic
387 BC	Plato	Socrates	monotheistic
344 BC	Aristotle	Plato	monotheistic
301 BC	Epicurus	Nausiphanes	atheistic?
293 BC	Zeno of Citium	Crates	monotheistic
290 BC	Euhemerus	?	historical

A centaur fighting a Lapith. Metope from Parthenon, about 440 BC.

SOME CONCLUSIONS

As can be seen above, there is really not anyone of the philosophers herein, who is unable to question the myths and the gods. Almost all of them show a significant amount of doubt, if not outright disbelief. They are willing to credit the gods with some kind of relevance, but far from the anthropomorphic existence portrayed in Homer and Hesiod.

Instead, they see them as costumed representations of natural forces, or as historical figures deified by posterity, or as plausible creatures somewhere in the cosmos, but with little power and no significant function. Such gods are more pitiful than awe-inspiring. And the myths about those gods are frowned upon by most philosophers.

Still, the philosophers see great and mysterious events in a primordial past, and cherish these events as readily as the pious do their gods. Natural forces and cosmic principles are sacred in the eyes of the philosophers, maybe to the extent that the philosophers do not regard them as substitutes for the divine, but its real essence. To the philosophers, each element is just as majestic, whatever mythical figure represents it, and no such impersonation can shade the glory of nature itself at work. In the eyes of most of the philosophers, nature itself is as divine as anything ever gets.

In that way, the philosophers probably regarded themselves as no less pious than those Greeks who actually believed in the gods of Homer and Hesiod.

On the other hand, since all the philosophers were clearly able to doubt the myths and the gods, so must any member of that society have been. Although praised through time in the whole western world, the philosophers were not a separate species. What their minds could conceive, any other mind would be able to perceive. Surely also, others than the philosophers could by themselves reach similar doubts.

This may be a non-controversial conclusion, almost a truism. Of course the Greeks were able to doubt their myths, and did so to some extent. But in the study of myth and gods in other cultures than our own, we tend to take for granted that the population is homogenous in trusting and believing the myths completely. Even if it is considered that other societies can relate to their myths in the ambiguous way the Greeks did, the consequences of this are not studied.

There are vast consequences regarding relations to the sacred, conceptions of the world, ethics, worship and ritual. If it is all done with an inkling of disbelief, where some minds question its framework, then that's quite another matter than blind trust.

If believing in the myths is not a prerequisite, then it is quite possible that this is not at all a vital function of theirs. They are stories, let's say a genre, and essentially have the same function as any other story: a kind of entertainment, enjoyment or thrill. The gods, then, are the characters in the stories, portrayed larger than life to enhance the thrill. They can be compared to the superheroes of modern day adventure stories. They are not believed to be real, but they bring a sense of wonder and amazement to the stories, making the audience feel that it would be spectacular if they were true.

If so, myths should primarily be studied as stories.

The gods, though, were not only characters in the wond-rous stories about them. They were also keys to basic cosmol-ogical components. The gods participated in the creation of the world, and they continued to be responsible for certain dynamics in it. This is seen by their relation to natural ele-ments and heavenly bodies. It is implied already in Hesiod's *Theogony*, where gods represent the Earth, Time, Air, and so on.

The Greek philosophers and historians tended to focus on this aspect of the gods – their symbolic connection to natural phenomena. When philosophers discussed the gods, they mostly considered the cosmological function the gods might or might not have. The mythological stories about them were peripheral to the philosophers, and rarely appre-ciated. But the links between the gods and certain cosmologi-cal concepts were treated at depth.

So, although the myths about the gods were stories, the gods themselves were primarily seen as keys to essential aspects of the cosmos. The Greek philosophers often gave the impression of following an ancient tradition in this attitude toward the gods, as if these were nothing but cosmological principles already from the moment of their appearance in human awareness.

Maybe the *theoi* that we translate as gods should more rightly be explained as *principles*. The gods were represen-tations of cosmological or other worldly principles, only later to be the subjects of devotion and festivity.

If so, some of the stories about the gods could be inter-preted as explanations and elaborations as to their functions in the cosmos. At least with the myth about the world's creation, this perspective is close at hand. The order of emergence of the gods represents the order in which the parts of the world came to be, and the genealogy of the gods shows what cosmic forces gave birth to others, and so on. In the minds of the Greek philosophers, surely, this was a much more inspiring perspective than that of the poets and their dramas, where the gods behaved just as human beings do.

Not only philosophers would hesitate to worship the gods by merit of their deeds in the myths of Homer and Hesiod alone. Therefore it is possible that all the Greeks primarily worshiped the gods for what they represented in a cosmological perspective, and not for the calamities they caused in the myths. The roles they played in the cosmos were what made them gods. The rest was entertainment.

If the word *theos*, god, has its roots in the holy and the festive, then what was regarded as holy was the world itself – existence – and that was what was celebrated. Through their gods, people glorified their own existence. We are still doing it.

THE PHILOSOPHERS

The School of Athens, by Raphael 1509 (detail). Plato and Aristotle are in the center, Diogenes lies on the stairs, Heraclitus sits by a desk in the foreground.

THALES
Flourished c. 584 BC.

Thales.

The earliest cosmological theories of an ancient Greek philosopher, would be those of Thales of Miletus (circa 624-546 BC), honored by his later peers as the very first philosopher and one of the Seven Sages. He flourished around 584 BC.[44]

By stating that the world had been formed out of the one substance water, he renounced the mythological accounts of how it all began. He replaced divine action with natural processes, where no gods were responsible for what took place. Yet, Aristotle claims that Thales saw the gods being present in everything, filling it somewhat like an ether or inner substance. Again according to Aristotle, Thales regarded also the lifeless things as having a soul. He used the magnet's influence on iron as an argument for his case, which Aristotle interpreted as the explanation to Thales' idea that god is in all.[45]

---

[44] Flourishing, *acme*, is traditionally used in dating the pre-Socratic philosophers, and equals their fortieth year of living.

[45] Aristotle, *de Anima*, 405a and 411a.

Furthermore, Thales may have been the first to maintain the soul's immortality.[46]

According to Diogenes Laertius he had stated that:

Of all things that are, the most ancient is God, for he is uncreated. [47]

Thales also made it clear that this eternal god was the creator of the world:

The most beautiful is the universe, for it is God's workmanship.[48]

If Diogenes is to be trusted, Thales expressed a firm monotheistic opinion. This is enforced by the impression of Aristotle that the divine of Thales is present in all, and not divided into separate divinities. He may not even have made a distinction between the divine and the soul. He claimed, again according to Diogenes Laertius, that there is not even any difference between life and death.[49] None of his own writing remains.

From what is known about Thales, he seems to have argued for a cosmology quite different from Greek mythology. So, already the very first of the Greek philosophers

[46] Diogenes Laertius, *Lives of Eminent Philosophers*, translated by R. D. Hicks, volume I, Loeb, London 1942, p.25.

[47] Diogenes Laertius, volume I, p.37.

[48] Diogenes Laertius, volume I, p.37.

[49] Diogenes Laertius, volume I, p.37.

reasoned independently of the heritage from Homer and Hesiod. There is a vast distance between the monstrous primordial battles of the *Theogony*, and a single creator god, alone in existing before the world.

What more this eternal god may have done to the world, except create it, is unclear. It is possible that Thales regarded this god as a sort of creative essence, present in every piece of the world, an essence without which things would cease to exist.

ANAXIMANDER

Flourished c. 570 BC.

Anaximander. Mosaic (Rheinisches Landesmuseum, Trier).

Anaximander (circa 610-546 BC) was one of the earliest known Greek philosophers, only about a quarter century junior to Thales. To Anaximander, the boundless,[50] *apeiron*, was a basic principle of the world. The parts of it may be changing but as a whole it remains the same, eternally. He did not give this boundless an element or other significant character. This was something else:

> *it is neither water nor any other of the so-called elements, but some different, boundless nature, from which all the heavens arise.*[51]

[50] A more accurate translation of the term Anaximander uses should be "what cannot be passed over or traversed from end to end." Kahn, Charles H., *Anaximander and the Origins of Greek Cosmology*, New York 1960, p.232. In the Loeb 1942 edition of Diogenes Laertius, the word used is "unlimited" (volume I, p.131).

[51] Kahn, p.166.

Out of this, all existing things were formed as well as destroyed, "according to what must needs be; for they make amends and give reparations to one another for their offense, according to the ordinance of time."[52]

Aristotle points out that the boundless of Anaximander could not have any beginning, or it would have a limit. Thereby follows also that it cannot change significantly, in its own essence. But all the things of the world can change, and have done so since their formation. In Anaximander's cosmogony, the boundless was first. Out of the boundless, the world was formed when the qualities of hot and cold arose:

Something capable of generating Hot and Cold was separated off from the eternal (Boundless) in the formation of this world, and a sphere of fire from this source grew around the air about the earth like bark around a tree. When this sphere was torn off and closed up into certain circles, the sun and moon and stars came into being.[53]

Anaximander regarded the sea as a remaining first moisture, not dried up by the fire of the world formation. He seemed to believe that the sun continues to dry up the seas, so that in the future the Earth would be barren.[54] Animals at first arose from the primeval moisture, later to move toward drier land, changing shape in the process – as did man: "In

[52] Kahn, p.166.

[53] Kahn, p.85f.

[54] Kahn, p.102f.

the beginning man was similar to a different animal, namely, a fish."[55] About the Earth he stated:

The earth is aloft, not dominated by anything; it remains in place because of the similar distance from all points.[56]

Aristotle was deeply appreciative to this argument for why the Earth did not seem to move at all, without being held by something else. He explained it: "a thing established in the middle, with a similar relationship to the extremes, has no reason to move up rather than down or laterally; but since it cannot proceed in opposite directions at the same time, it will necessarily remain where it is."[57]

The same is expressed by Socrates in Plato's *Phaedo*, where he says that he is "persuaded", probably referring to the thoughts of Anaximander: "since the earth is round and in the middle of the heaven, it has no need either of Air or any other Necessity in order not to fall, but the similarity of the heaven to itself in every way and the equilibrium of the earth suffice to hold it still."[58]

Regarding the shape of the Earth, though, Anaximander saw it as a cylinder, "with a depth one third of its width".[59]

Diogenes Laertius has little to say about Anaximander, and makes no reference to any book of his, only "a sum-

[55] Kahn, p.110.
[56] Kahn, p.76.
[57] Kahn, p.76.
[58] Kahn, p.79.
[59] Kahn, p.81.

mary" of his doctrines that later thinkers got hold of. The astronomical theories of Anaximander, Diogenes seems to have mixed up with those of Anaxagoras.[60]

Anaximander's universe needed none of the divine forces acting in the myths of Homer and Hesiod. We have no statement of his regarding their existence, but their complete absence from his cosmology hints an atheistic view, or at least one where the gods have little to do with the fundamental processes of the world. These processes are instead given a mechanical order that could be called astronomical, in the sense that the forces at work are contained within the universe and its natural substances.

[60] Diogenes Laertius, *Lives of Eminent Philosophers*, translated by R. D. Hicks, volume I, Loeb, London 1942, p. 131.

ANAXIMENES
Flourished c. 545 BC.

Anaximenes.

Anaximenes (circa 585-528 BC), the pupil of Anaximander, specified his teacher's *apeiron*, the boundless, to have the element air. To him, air was the substance of which all was made, also the gods and things divine.

He regarded air as this all encompassing ether, because: "Air is near to the incorporeal"[61] Also, it is never exhausted, though every living creature is generated by breathing it.

When the air is uniform it is not visible, but when set in motion, when turning hot or cold, or when moistened, it gets perceivable shapes. It is always moving and changing, or there would not be so many things forming in it. When dissolved, it becomes fire, when compressed water, and when further condensed earth, lastly stone, its most condensed form.[62]

[61] Freeman, Kathleen, *Ancilla to The Pre-Socratic Philosophers*, Oxford 1952, p.19.

[62] Kahn, Charles H., *Anaximander and the Origins of Greek Cosmology*, New York 1960, p.149.

The soul, too, is air, and that which keeps the body intact. The 1ˢᵗ century BC philosopher Aetius quotes him stating:

> *As our soul, which is air, holds us together, so do breath and air surround the whole universe.*[63]

Like the cosmos of Anaximander, that of his pupil is in little need of the gods. The universe works by its own machinery, creating and upholding everything within it – including the gods. This is an astronomical order in no need of divine influence.

There are gods in his universe, but they are secondary, not elevated above the rest of creation. Thus, they are hardly gods at all. The universe of Anaximenes is ruled solely by the element air and its movement.

Diogenes Laertius has very little to say about Anaximenes, and quotes him only with two letters of little significance to his philosophy. Both are written to Pythagoras. In the first of those letters he praises Thales, written at the time of his passing. The second tells of imminent war and how this upsets him:

> *How then can Anaximenes any longer think of studying the heavens when threatened with destruction or slavery?*[64]

[63] Freeman, p.19.

[64] Diogenes Laertius, *Lives of Eminent Philosophers*, translated by R. D. Hicks, volume I, Loeb, London 1942, p. 135.

PYTHAGORAS
Flourished c. 542 BC.

Pythagoras.

To Pythagoras (circa 582-500 BC), the gods were both factual and worthy of reverence, if later commentators are to be trusted. Nothing remains of his own words. According to the 4th century BC historian Hieronymus, Pythagoras descended into Hades, where:

> *he saw the soul of Hesiod bound fast to a brazen pillar and gibbering, and the soul of Homer hung on a tree with serpents writhing about it, this being their punishment for what they had said about the gods.*[65]

What upset Pythagoras, as well as several other philosophers, was the brutality, immorality and other flaws of character, of which the gods showed plenty in the works of Homer and Hesiod.

[65] Diogenes Laertius, *Lives of Eminent Philosophers*, translated by R. D. Hicks, volume II, Loeb, London 1950, p.339.

Pythagoras' teaching was strict and full of rules to live by, some of which were expressions of piety, and some were rather peculiar. He was secretive with his teaching and demanded much of those who wanted to be his disciples. Among other things, they had to wait for long before being accepted.

Not only did he avoid meat, but for several reasons he refused beans, to the extent that he was reported to have died because of it: When fleeing from his enemies he stopped before a field of beans, unwilling to cross it. Thereby, he was caught and killed.

Diogenes Laertius writes that "his disciples held the opinion about him that he was Apollo come down from the far north."[66] Pythagoras himself had no less a view on his person. According to the 4th century philosopher Heraclides of Pontus, he said about himself that he was the son of Hermes, who had offered him any gift except immortality. "So he asked to retain through life and through death a memory of his experiences."[67] Thus, his soul wandered from person to person, all of them noble men, keeping its memory through each new life lived. To Pythagoras, this was nothing extraordinary, since:

> *He was the first, they say, to declare that the soul, bound now in this creature, now in that, thus goes on a round ordained of necessity.*[68]

[66] Diogenes Laertius, volume II, p.331.

[67] Diogenes Laertius, volume II, p.323.

[68] Diogenes Laertius, volume II, p.333.

This is, in essence, identical with the *metempsychosis* of Pherecydes, who is most likely to have preceded Pythagoras in expressing the theory.

This wandering of the soul was not exclusive to man, nor was the soul itself. Pythagoras avoided meat, and "forbade even the killing, let alone the eating, of animals which share with us the privilege of having a soul."[69]

From Alexander Polyhistor's 1st century BC book *Successions of Philosophers*, Diogenes Laertius receives the mathematical cosmology of Pythagoras:

The principle of all things is the monad or unit; arising from this monad the undefined dyad or two serves as material substratum to the monad, which is cause; from the monad and the undefined dyad spring numbers; from numbers, points; from points, lines; from lines, plane figures; from plane figures, solid figures; from solid figures, sensible bodies, the elements of which are four, fire, water, earth and air; these elements interchange and turn into one another completely, and combine to produce a universe animate, intelligent, spherical, with the earth at its centre, the earth itself too being spherical and inhabited round about. There are also antipodes, and our 'down' is their 'up'.[70]

[69] Diogenes Laertius, volume II, p.333.
[70] Diogenes Laertius, volume II, p.343.

Such a strictly ordered universe has little room for gods and their adventurous ways of creating the world, as told by Hesiod. Though Pythagoras fondled mythological ingredients in his relation to himself and his calling, in his cosmology he replaced them with principles of higher purity and precision: numbers and their relations, rather than anthropomorphic creatures.

The Pythagoreans, his followers, frequently used allegorical concepts for essential matters in their teachings, claiming this practice to stem directly from their founder.[71] If indeed their master did the same, mythology could to him have been nothing but a colorful way of expressing his theories. Then his mathematical cosmogony would rightly be categorized as an atheist one.

Still, he must have given some meaning to the gods, or he would not have been so upset by Homer and Hesiod. If he had an allegorical use for the gods, he may have objected to myths about them for the reason that those myths obstructed the symbols he had the gods be.

Certainly, there is reverence of some kind in the way he presents his very orderly universe. Whether the gods were real or not to him, he wanted them to conform to that order.

[71] Freeman, Kathleen, *The Pre-Socratic Philosophers*, Oxford 1946, p.254.

PHERECYDES OF SYROS
Flourished c. 540 BC.[72]

Pherecydes.

Pherecydes (circa 580-? BC) is traditionally credited to be the teacher of Pythagoras, although a couple of years his junior. According to the 4th century historian Theopompus – and Cicero[73] – he was the first to write in the Greek language about nature and the gods.[74] One of those texts was *Hepta-mychos*, on the origin of the world, remaining only in fragments.

He is likely to have been the first to proclaim the immortality of the soul, if not second to Thales, and the originator of the principle of *metempsychosis*, the immortal human soul

---

[72] This year of flourishing is given in Diogenes Laertius, volume I, p. 121. Diogenes does himself not specify the year, only that Pherecydes "lived in the 59th Olympiad", which was 544-541 BC (p. 1.) Britannica.com gives the year of flourishing c. 550 BC.

[73] Schibli, Hermann S., *Pherekydes of Syros*, Oxford 1990, p.142f.

[74] Diogenes Laertius, *Lives of Eminent Philosophers*, translated by R. D. Hicks, volume I, Loeb, London 1942, p.122f.

passing from one body to the next – human or animal – after the death of the flesh.

The beginning of the world was to him the elements fire, air and water springing from Cronus. Diogenes Laertius quotes the start of a book of his:

Zeus and Time and Earth were from all eternity.[75]

By this he clearly opposed the primordial chaos of Hesiod, instead to be more in line with a number of pre-Socratic philosophers who stated the importance of recognizing something eternal, neither ever born nor ever dying.[76]

Those three primary and eternal deities are Zeus, Cronus and Chthonie, and of them it is Cronus who does, by his own seed, produce the three elements fire, breath (air) and water. From the elements a multitude of additional gods are born.[77] In *Derision of Gentile Philosophers*, Hermias explains the cosmogony of Pherecydes in this manner:

Pherecydes says the principles are Zen and Chthonie and Cronus; Zen is the aither, Chthonie the earth and Cronus is time; the aither is that which acts, the earth is that which is acted upon, time is that in which events come to pass.[78]

[75] Diogenes Laertius, p.125.

[76] Schibli, p.15. Schibli has chosen not to use the latin spelling of Greek names.

[77] Schibli, p.14 and 163.

[78] Schibli, p.165.

Zen is Zeus, by Pherecydes spelled in many differing ways. Says Herodian, the grammarian of the 3rd century CE:

I am not unaware that God is variously spoken of by the ancients. For there is also Dis and Zen and Den and Zas and Zes in Pherecydes according to his own inflection.[79]

Aristotle argued that Pherecydes, calling him a theologian, was mixing philosophical reasoning with myth in stating that the god Zeus would be the original ruler.[80]

When Pherecydes makes the three gods Zen, Cronus and Chthonie eternal, he seems to be stating what needs to be present for a world to be created at all, the very basics of nature: aither (aether), earth and time – similar to the later ideas of space, matter and time. There had to be a space in which the world could appear, some substance to form it, and time in which it would commence to exist.

This mixture, where the gods represent fundamental forces of nature, could also be called allegorical, in the sense used about mythology, where gods and myths about them represent certain meanings or events, other than those described. Pherecydes comes the closest to this use of the gods.

[79] Schibli, p.163f.

[80] Aristotle, *Metaphysics*, 1091a29-b 12, quoted in Schibli, p.171.

XENOPHANES
Flourished 530 BC.

Xenophanes.

Xenophanes of Colophon (570-478 BC) spoke out against the mythology of Homer and Hesiod, to the point of being scorned by Timon: "Xenophanes, not over-proud, perverter of Homer, castigator."[81] Diogenes Laertius explains that he wrote, in three different metre, verses "attacking Hesiod and Homer and denouncing what they said about the gods."[82] Xenophanes blamed them for having "ascribed unto the Gods all that is reproach and blame in the world of men, stealing and adultery and deceit."[83]

Xenophanes had no patience with the concept of a multitude of gods, accredited with distinct and often unsympathetic anthropomorphic features. It was clear to him that gods are given the countenance of their worshipers:

---

[81] Diogenes Laertius, *Lives of Eminent Philosophers*, translated by R. D. Hicks, volume II, Loeb, London 1950, p.425.

[82] Diogenes Laertius, volume II, p.427.

[83] Edmonds, J. M., *Elegy and Iambus*, volume I, Loeb, London, 1932, p.201.

The Aethiop saith that his Gods are snub-nosed and black, the Thracian that his have blue eyes and red hair.[84]

He finds it likely that if bulls or horses had hands and could paint, they would portray the gods with horse or bull features.[85] Thereby it is evident that he regarded much about the gods as coming out of human imagination. To him there was only one god, lacking any human trait. According to Diogenes Laertius, Xenophanes claimed:

The substance of God is spherical, in no way resembling man. He is all eye and all ear, but does not breathe; he is the totality of mind and thought, and is eternal.[86]

Except for this god, who is eternal, anything that has come into being is doomed to perish. The soul, Xenophanes regarded simply as breath.[87]

Xenophanes' cosmology is clearly a monotheistic one, where the one god is distanced from the world and its mortal inhabitants. Not only does this god lack any resemblance with living beings, but seems to have little to do with them at all. The god of Xenophanes is best described as the very principle of immortality, of eternity, and nothing else.

[84] Edmonds, p.203.

[85] Edmonds, p.201.

[86] Diogenes Laertius, volume II, p.427.

[87] Diogenes Laertius, volume II, p.427.

THEAGENES

Flourished c. 525 BC.

Wrestling with the unwillingness common among philosophers to accept that illustrious gang of gods in the works
of Homer and Hesiod, Theagenes of Rhegium (circa 565-?
BC) was the first to find a clearly allegorical way of reading
the myths. They were to be understood as expressions of
natural forces.

The battles of the gods, as Homer and Hesiod described
them, were really wars of the elements and fundamental
qualities of the world, as they related to one another in
opposites – fire against water, hot against cold, light against
heavy.

In this menagerie, fire was represented by Apollo, Helios
and Hephaestus, water by Poseidon and Scamander, air by
Hera, and so forth. Also abstract qualities had divine repre-
sentation – wisdom with Athene, desire with Aphrodite,
reason with Hermes and folly, no less, with Ares.[88] For gods
to actually do battle, in the way Homer and Hesiod have it,
would be unbecoming to them.

No writing of his own remains, nor any fragments of his
words. Diogenes Laertius does not write about him or
include him in his listings of Greek philosophers. He is

---

[88] Freeman, Kathleen, *The Pre-Socratic Philosophers*, Oxford 1946, p.41.

known to us for little else than his interpretation of the myths.

Theagenes' allegorical ideas can be compared to those of Empedocles. See the text on Empedocles for a comparison of the two.

Zeus throwing a lightning bolt. Sculpture from the 4ᵗʰ century BC.

HECATAEUS
Flourished c. 510 BC.

Hecataeus of Miletus (Hekataios, circa 550-476 BC) was by Herodotus called a historian. He wrote an early history and a book on his travels. He also pioneered in distinguishing between myth and historical fact, which did not stop him from claiming to be of divine blood, according to Herodotus in *Histories*: "Hecataeus had traced his descent and claimed that his sixteenth forefather was a god."[89]

This he told the priests of Zeus in Thebes, who responded by showing their descent by the small figures preserved in the temple, each made by one ancestor – all in all 345 of them. The priests said that none of them had been a god, but each and everyone a *Piromis*, in all respects a good man.

Otherwise, Hecataeus distanced himself considerably from the spectacles of the myths. He commences his book *Genealogia*:

> *Hecataeus of Miletus thus speaks: I write what I deem true; for the stories of the Greeks are manifold and seem to me ridiculous.*

[89] Herodotus, *Histories*, 2.143.4, volume I, translated by A. D. Godley, Loeb, London 1981, p.451.

Regarding the sober way Hecataeus had of seeing through myth, the 2nd century CE geographer Pausanias gives an example in his *Description of Greece*. It concerns Taenarum, where "some of the Greek poets" claimed that Heracles had raised the hounds of Hades:

> But Hecataeus of Miletus gave a plausible explanation, stating that a terrible serpent lived on Taenarum, and was called the hound of Hades, because any one bitten was bound to die of the poison at once, and it was this snake, he said, that was brought by Heracles to Eurystheus. But Homer, who was the first to call the creature brought by Heracles the hound of Hades, did not give it a name or describe it as of manifold form, as he did in the case of the Chimaera. Later poets gave the name Cerberus, and though in other respects they made him resemble a dog, they say that he had three heads. Homer, however, does not imply that he was a dog, the friend of man, any more than if he had called a real serpent the hound of Hades.[90]

His historical work, *Genealogia* or *Historiai*, remains only in a few fragments, but is regarded as having systematically presented Greek tradition and myth.

It is not clear what he believed or disbelieved about the gods, but he obviously allowed himself to doubt the myths about them. This implies a materialistic view on the world,

---

[90] Pausanias, *Description of Greece*, Laconia, translated by W.H.S. Jones and H.A. Ormerod, London 1918, 3.25.5-6.

where wondrous events and creatures are highly unlikely, if not completely impossible. Since he preferred to see historical events behind the myths, that is how I classify him.

HERACLITUS
Flourished c. 502 BC.[91]

Heraclitus.

Heraclitus (Herakleitos, circa 542-480 BC) is famous for the expression *panta rhei*, all things flow, and for his cryptic way of expressing his thoughts, as well as his consistently bad mood and obnoxious comments. He thought that Homer "ought by rights to be ejected from the lists and thrashed" for his weak understanding of cosmological matters,[92] and no higher was his opinion on Hesiod:

> *For very many people Hesiod is (their) teacher. They are certain he knew a great number of things – he who continually failed to recognize (even) day and night (for what they are)! For they are one.*[93]

[91] Diogenes Laertius says the 69th Olympiad, which was 504-501 BC. Diogenes Laertius, *Lives of Eminent Philosophers*, translated by R. D. Hicks, volume II, Loeb, London 1950, p.409.

[92] Robinson, T. M., *Heraclitus: Fragments*, Toronto 1987, p.33 and 108f.

[93] Robinson, p.39 and 120f.

Hesiod said that night "produced" day, whereas to Heraclitus there is no more difference between the two than the lack of sunlight in the former.

The worship of the gods he found outright mad. People believed themselves to be purified with the blood from sacrifice, "as if one who had stepped into mud should wash himself off with mud", and that was not all:

> *Furthermore, they pray to these statues – as though one were to carry on a conversation with houses.*[94]

Though it is clear that he saw nothing divine neither in these practices nor their objects of worship, Heraclitus recognized something of divine nature as well as something moral, judgmental, in the cosmos. He did not accept a multitude of gods, but one, although with many names and different qualities:

> *God (is) day (and) night, winter (and) summer, war (and) peace, satiety (and) famine, and undergoes change in the way that (fire?), whenever it is mixed with spices, gets called by the name that accords with (the) bouquet of each.*[95]

Instead of "fire" in this fragment of his works, interpreters have also suggested "air", "myrrh" or "olive oil".[96] What

---

[94] Robinson, p.13.

[95] Robinson, p.45.

[96] Robinson, p.128f.

seems most likely in the drastic comparison between a single god's spread over celestial opposites on the one hand, and the bouquet of spices on the other, would be something in the line of olive oil. That would also be in line with Heraclitus' drastic way of expressing his thoughts.

Heraclitus does give fire a central place:

Fire, having come suddenly upon all things, will judge and convict them.[97]

Although to the 3rd century Christian writer Hippolytus this seemed to point directly to the fires of hell and a punishing god, it should rather be interpreted as a cosmological statement,[98] since Heraclitus also stated:

To god all things are fair and just, whereas humans have supposed that some things are unjust, other things just.[99]

The god of Heraclitus is of cosmological nature, a natural order, not bothering with human affairs – somewhat the same as the all-encompassing meaning his interpreters have given to his use of the word *logos*. This god seems as abstract as a formula, not in any way a personality with a will of its own, not even responsible for making the world, which to Heraclitus is:

---

[97] Robinson, p.45.

[98] Robinson, p.127.

[99] Robinson, p.61.

the same for all, no god or man made, but it always was,
is, and will be, an ever living fire, being kindled in meas-
ures and being put out in measures.[100]

This is an automatic cosmos, governed only by its own natural laws, where fire is the basic element and its dynamics are what make things appear as well as dissolve. This grand, eternal process is completely impersonal:

Things grasped together: things whole, things not whole;
being brought together, being separated; consonant, dis-
sonant. Out of all things one thing, and out of one thing
all things.[101]

Another fragment has him simply state:

All things are one.[102]

When man accredits meaning to it all, and traces a higher will in what takes place and how things behave, he is merely fondling illusions. He is dreaming. And dreaming evidently intrigues Heraclitus. The strange difference between being asleep and awake addresses what the world really is:

[100] Robinson, p.25.
[101] Robinson, p.15.
[102] Robinson, p.37.

for those who are awake there is a single, common uni-
verse, whereas in sleep each person turns away into (his)
own, private (universe).[103]

The implication of those opposite states of mind goes
further:

A person in (the) night kindles a light for himself, since
his vision has been extinguished. In his sleep he touches
that which is dead, though (himself) alive, when awake
touches that which sleeps.[104]

This cryptic fragment has been interpreted in several
directions, sometimes so that night signifies the night of
death.[105] Also when read more directly, it shows how Heraclitus marvels at the border of being awake and asleep,
implying clues to what death may be. He shares this bewil-
derment with countless thinkers and cultures all through
human existence. Our dreaming forces us to question what
reality really is.

Death fascinates this somber man. He does not claim to
understand it, but to see its vast significance:

There await people when they die things they neither
expect nor imagine.[106]

[103] Robinson, p.55.

[104] Robinson, p.23.

[105] Robinson, p.93f.

[106] Robinson, p.23.

Here he voices a firm distrust in what the myths have to say about the realm of death, but also the appreciation of the question's obtrusive importance to each and everyone.

He still dares to state something about death, but this is in relation to his view on the elements of the cosmos. The soul, he claims, is made up of water, and therefore: "for souls it is death to become water", in the same way as it is death for water to become earth, out of which it has come into existence.[107]

This does not mean that the soul, by many philosophers compared to air, would to Heraclitus be water. But it emanates from water, much like vapor.[108] Nor does it mean that he regards death as final. But from his words on the matter, here and in other fragments, it is at least clear that he is not convinced of an afterlife, of whatever nature.[109]

He treats immortality mostly as a paradox:

Immortals mortal, mortals immortal, these living the death of those, those dead in the life of these.[110]

This saying has been discussed as to its meaning. Although the expression *immortals* was generally used by the

---

[107] Robinson, p.29.

[108] Water is quite damaging to the soul, according to Heraclitus. For example, the drunken man stumbles because his soul is wet. Robinson, p.69.

[109] Robinson, p.104f.

[110] Robinson, p.43.

Greek for their gods, this needs not be the case here.[111] What Heraclitus states, no doubt, is the uncertainty of it all – life ending or not, death real or not, a puzzle impossible to solve. If it refers to the gods being alive only in the imaginations of the people, then the immortals are mortal in the sense that they die when the people believing in them do, and at the same time people dreaming of eternal gods do in a sense make themselves immortal, if only in this way, akin to a dream.

Heraclitus is vague on those grand matters, because he is uncertain, and what he can state firmly is little but the disillusioning fact that none can know any better. The world being such an uncertain thing, illusive and elusive, his research found a single means:

I investigated myself.[112]

It did not make him jolly.

According to Diogenes Laertius, Heraclitus had no teacher, but "inquired of himself". The same source mentions that some have Xenophanes as his teacher – if so, he was hardly a pupil loyal to his master's thoughts.[113] His attitude to intellectual feats was not that respectful at all. Diogenes quotes him saying:

---

[111] Robinson, p.124f.

[112] Robinson, p.61.

[113] Diogenes Laertius, volume II, p. 413.

Much learning does not teach understanding; else would it have taught Hesiod and Pythagoras, or, again, Xenophanes and Hecataeus.[114]

He preferred to play knucklebones with young boys at the temple of Artemis.[115]

His cosmology is definitely a monotheistic one. He rejects the gods of Homer and Hesiod without the least hesitation, and enjoys doing it. Considering the determination with which he denounces the mythology of his fellow men, it is surprising that his cosmology is not a completely atheistic one.

---

[114] Diogenes Laertius, volume II, p. 409.

[115] Diogenes Laertius, volume II, p. 411.

PARMENIDES
Flourished c. 475 BC.[116]

Parmenides.

Parmenides (circa 515-450 BC) seems not to have held any strong belief in the gods, certainly not in the anthropomorphic forms Homer and Hesiod had them appear. Instead he made allegorical interpretations of the myths, much like Theagenes had done in the century before, and Empedocles did in his own time. Yet, it was none other than the goddess Dike herself, who declared to him what grand mission he was to engage upon:

> *It is necessary that you shall learn all things, as well the unshaken heart of well-rounded truth as the opinions of mortals in which there is no true belief.*[117]

---

[116] Diogenes Laertius claims that Parmenides flourished in the 69th Olympiad, that is 504-500 BC. Diogenes Laertius, *Lives of Eminent Philosophers*, translated by R. D. Hicks, volume II, Loeb, London 1950, p. 433. Most experts claim a later date to be more likely.

[117] Tarán, Leonardo, *Parmenides: A Text with Translation, Commentary, and Critical Essays*, Princeton 1965, p.9.

Parmenides doubted the senses, and insisted that only reason should be trusted.[118]

Tradition has it that he was a pupil of Xenophanes, although few of their ideas match. Some have said that he was connected to the Pythagoreans, who were partly near to his ways of reasoning through mathematical deduction.[119]

Following his own reasoning, the gods must somehow exist, because people are able to imagine them. He argued:

> *For you could not know that which does not exist (because it is impossible) nor could you express it.*[120]

The nature of being and non-being is the center of his attention, to the extent of pure agitation:

> *It is necessary to say and to think Being; for there is Being, but nothing is not. These things I order you to ponder.*[121]

Mortals are confused on this point, he claims, a confusion that may very well be impossible to straighten out:

> *They are carried deaf and blind at the same time, amazed, a horde incapable of judgement, by whom to be and not*

---

[118] Diogenes Laertius, volume II, p. 431.

[119] Tarán, p.3.

[120] Tarán, p.32.

[121] Tarán, p.54.

to be are considered the same and yet not the same, for
whom the path of all things is backward-turning.[122]

The mythology and beliefs of his fellow men must to Parmenides have been a striking evidence of this, since the absurdities of the gods and their doings had been pointed out already before his days. This led him to a firm cosmological view, where what is must always have been, since it cannot have come out of non-being:

Thus it is necessary to exist all in all or not at all.[123]

Therefore, when he talked about the ether and the "pure torch of the resplendent sun" coming into being,[124] he must have been referring to a process of change, and not any kind of *creatio ex nihilo* (creation out of nothing). This is implied by his saying that the Earth, sun and moon, the ether, the stars and the outermost Olympus "strove eagerly to come into being."[125]

Just as being and non-being is a pair of opposites, he saw such dynamic counterparts making up the processes of the cosmos – from the pair of Light and Night which equally fill all things,[126] to that of man and woman. But there is a one,

---

[122] Tarán, p.54.

[123] Tarán, p.85.

[124] Tarán, p.165.

[125] Tarán, p.166.

[126] Tarán, p.161.

not herself the counterpart to anyone or anything, in charge of it all:

In the middle of these is the goddess who governs all things. For everywhere she is the beginner of union and of painful birth, sending the female to unite with the male and again to the contrary the male with the female.[127]

She is also the one to have "devised Eros as the very first of all gods."[128]

The sun is splendid in the mind of Parmenides, whereas he states about the moon that its light is but a reflection of that of the sun: "Wandering around the earth shining in the night with a borrowed light."[129] About the Earth he may have been the first to express the opinion that it is spherical, though not in those actual fragments of his texts remaining.[130]

Parmenides stands out in clearly stating the highest divinity to be female. Although Hesiod implies the same in giving Gaia, the Earth goddess, a central role in the world's creation, most Greek thinkers imagine a male supreme god, if giving it any gender.

Diogenes Laertius explains that Parmenides had two elements at work in his cosmology: fire and earth. The

[127] Tarán, p.166.

[128] Tarán, p.168. In Greek mythology, there are two concepts of Eros: a primeval god of nature, and the love god similar to the Roman god Cupid.

[129] Tarán, p.168.

[130] Tarán, p.296ff.

former should be understood as the craftsman, and the latter as his material.[131] This symbolic use of elements is far from unique among Greek philosophers. Surely Parmenides saw fire and earth as counterparts, just as he did with light and dark, hot and cold, and so on. The meeting of these counterparts was the melting pot of creation.

In Plato's dialogue *Parmenides*, two things are discussed at depth: the Socratic idealism and the concept of the one as opposed to the many. Plato shows great respect for Parmenides in this dialogue. Such kindness was not often the case for others than Socrates, in Plato's writing.[132]

There is a divine grandness in the cosmology of Parmenides, although the gods are transformed into philosophical principles, very far indeed from the characters of Homer and Hesiod. He insists that the gods should be understood in an allegorical way, but also that they are gods, nonetheless.

---

[131] Diogenes Laertius, volume II, p. 431.

[132] Plato, *Parmenides*.

ANAXAGORAS

Flourished c. 460 BC.

Anaxagoras. Illustration in a book of later date.

Anaxagoras (circa 500-428 BC) was a pupil of Anaximenes, and according to Diogenes Laertius: "the first who set mind above matter." He quoted the beginning of what might be the only book Anaxagoras wrote:

> *All things were together; then came Mind and set them in order.*[133]

Therefore, according to the same source, he was given the nickname *Nous*, mind. No nickname could honor him more, since *Nous* was to Anaxagoras a most elevated thing, like a god – and a monotheistic god at that. He saw the primordial world as a homogenous cluster, where everything in it was truly part of everything else, so that none was a separate, independent entity – except for Nous, reason, which was in no way part of that world:

---

[133] Diogenes Laertius, *Lives of Eminent Philosophers*, translated by R. D. Hicks, volume I, Loeb, London 1942, p.137.

While other things have a share of everything, Nous is infinite, self-governing, and has been mixed with nothing, but is alone unto itself.[134]

Separated this way, it was able to rule the world. It began the process of differentiation and development, by means of a revolving movement, starting in a small area and expanding. By this, the world started breaking up in smaller parts, whereby the heavenly bodies were born, warm was separated from cold, bright from dark, dry from moist. In this revolving movement, some things were separated and others joined. To Anaxagoras, this is really all that takes place in the world:

The Greeks do not employ (the words) 'coming to be' and 'perishing' correctly, for nothing comes into being or is even destroyed; rather, from (pre-) existing things there is combining and breaking up. They would, therefore, be correct to call coming-to-be 'combining' and perishing 'breaking up'.[135]

For Heaven and Earth, Anaxagoras saw their making as a mixing of qualities, giving each of the two its significance much in line with the Greek tradition, and certainly in many other traditions as well.

---

[134] Sider, David, *The Fragments of Anaxagoras*, Beiträge zur Klassischen Philologie 118, Hain 1981, p.94.

[135] Sider, p.119.

The dense and the moist and the cold and the dark came together here where the earth is now; the rare and the warm and the dry (and the bright) moved outward into the far-off limits of the aither.[136]

On the microscopic perspective he stated that there is no thing which is the smallest, since there can always be something smaller and no matter how small a part is, it cannot be cut away to nothing.[137]

Anaxagoras was tried in court, probably for declaring that the sun was a mass of red-hot metal, larger than Peloponnesus. He was expelled from Athens, where he had lived for 30 years.[138]

Evidently, Anaxagoras had little respect for the myths of Homer and Hesiod. In his cosmology, he was completely indifferent to and independent of them. His sole divinity, Nous, seems to have little to do with the world, except for commencing its creation. Perhaps it should be seen as a principle, a natural law on which the world was based. It is so impersonal that one could describe Anaxagoras' cosmos as an atheistic one, at least in comparison with the willful and self-aware creatures that others call gods.

[136] Sider, p.114.

[137] Sider, p.54.

[138] Diogenes Laertius comments, though, that there are other versions of what Anaxagoras was tried for, and the idea of the sun could come from Tantalus. Diogenes Laertius, volume I, p.143 and 137.

EMPEDOCLES
Flourished c. 450 BC.

Empedocles.

As for Empedocles (circa 490-430 BC), he saw the world as somewhat a battleground of two major forces: love, *Philia*, joining things together, and strife, *Neikos*, breaking them apart. To him the basic elements were four, each one bearing the name of a god – Zeus was fire, Hera was air, Aidoneus was earth and Nestis water:

> *Hear first the four roots of all things: bright Zeus and life-bringing Hera and Aidoneus and Nestis, whose tears are the source of mortal streams.*[139]

Love he also called joy, linking it to the goddess Aphrodite. To Empedocles, no god was in any way of human countenance:

---

[139] Wright, M. R., *Empedocles: the Extant Fragments*, New Haven 1981, p.164. There has been some discussion, already among Greek commentators, as to what element Empedocles meant each god to represent, but the above mentioned is today regarded as the most likely (p.165f).

For he is not equipped with a human head on a body, [two branches do not spring from his back], he has no feet, no swift knees, no shaggy genitals, but he is mind alone, holy and inexpressible, darting through the whole cosmos with swift thoughts.[140]

His poetic vision has a flare for magnificence – that of nature as well as that of himself.[141] Empedocles saw in this everlasting exchange between love and strife, between joining and separating, a beauty that is easy to appreciate:

And these things never cease their continual exchange of position, at one time all coming together into one through love, at another again being borne away from each other by strife's repulsion.[142]

He regarded both birth and death as illusions, misconceptions of the mixing and change taking place in the dynamics between love and strife. Therefore, he could easily embrace *metempsychosis*, the idea of the soul passing from one body to another – sometimes human, sometimes of another species:

[140] Wright, p.253. The line within brackets might not be authentic in this fragment.

[141] "I tell you I travel up and down as an immortal god, mortal no longer, honored by all it seems, crowned with ribbons and fresh garlands." Wright, p.264. Concerning his own death there are several traditions, some claiming he sought it himself, in such a fashion as to prove his divine nature.

[142] Wright, p.166.

Before now I was born a boy and a maid, a bush and a bird, and a dumb fish leaping out of the sea.[143]

He obviously saw comfort in this. Neither birth nor death existed to him:

Here is another point: of all mortal things no one has birth, or any end in pernicious death, but there is only mixing, and separating of what has been mixed, and to these men give the name 'birth'.[144]

His conviction of souls related across the boundaries of species, led him to firmly oppose the sacrifice of animals, as well as at all eating their meat:

Alas that the pitiless day did not destroy me first, before I devised for my lips the cruel deed of eating flesh.[145]

He saw in this nothing other than cannibalism, the eating of one's own kind, just as clearly as were the animals one's siblings or children:

[143] Diogenes Laertius, *Lives of Eminent Philosophers*, translated by R. D. Hicks, volume II, Loeb, London 1950, p.391.

[144] Wright, p.174f.

[145] Wright, p.284.

*Will you not cease from the din of slaughter? Do you not
see that you are devouring one another because of your
careless way of thinking?*[146]

Aristotle, presenting the cosmology of Empedocles in
straightforward words, has some objections to its inconsis-
tencies, claiming that often love breaks apart instead of joins,
and it can also happen that strife joins. What Aristotle sees as
the cause behind love and strife must be all good and all bad,
and thereby he finds it accurate to regard Empedocles as the
first of all to point out good and bad as primary causes.[147]

His allegorical interpretation of the gods as elements can
be compared to that of Theagenes, presented above. But they
do not agree completely on what god each element represents. Also, Theagenes did not include the element earth,
whereas Empedocles had it represented by Aidoneus. Theagenes was about 75 years senior to Empedocles, who seems
not to have related to the thoughts of the preceding philosopher, in spite of the similarities. He may not even have
known of him.

Gods related to the elements

Element	Theagenes	Empedocles
fire	Apollo, Helios, Hephaestus	Zeus
earth	–	Aidoneus
air	Hera	Hera
water	Poseidon, Scamander	Nestis

[146] Wright, p.285.

[147] Aristotle, *Metaphysics*, 984b-985a, translated by Hugh Lawson-Tancred, London 1998, p.14ff.

Empedocles' universe is a poetic one. The never-ending struggle between Love and Strife is another of the many cosmoses of opposites that mankind has figured out. We would in our time be more convenient, if that is the word, with Hate as the opposite to Love. Maybe Empedocles knew more about the foundation of hate than we do. Without strife, where would hate get its nourishment?

Although Empedocles' universe is a poetic one, it is distinctly different from that of Homer and Hesiod. The gods are the elements, and to Empedocles there is nothing more one needs to know about them. He seems to ignore the myths completely.

HERODOTUS
Flourished c. 450 BC.

Herodotus. Marble. Roman copy of a Greek early 4th century BC original.

The historian Herodotus (Herodotos, circa 490-425 BC) traveled extensively in the world known to the Greek at his time, spending what must have been many years on this. He finished writing his *History*, the book on so much more than the Greco-Persian wars and their preludes, no earlier than 430 BC. It seems to have been known before the year 425 BC.

Contrary to what is the case with most of the Greek literature of that time, his book is quite intact, with its rich information on the lands and lives of Greece and its neighboring states.

In a narrative form he treated foreigners no worse than his countrymen, sometimes actually praising the former at the expense of the latter. Contrary to the tradition, he avoided involving any divine interference, but showed the events of history as caused by human action.

Regarding the gods and the rites of their worship, he was convinced of practically all of it being imported from Egypt to Greece. He starts, almost discreetly, in the 49th chapter of the second book[148]:

> *For it was Melampus who taught the Greeks the name of Dionysus, and the way of sacrificing to him.*[149]

Next, in the following paragraph, he broadens the revelation immensely:

> *Indeed, wellnigh all the names of the gods came to Hellas from Egypt. For I am assured by inquiry that they have come from foreign parts, and I believe that they came chiefly from Egypt.*[150]

He lists some few exceptions: Poseidon, the Dioscuri, Hera, Hestia, Themis, the Graces and the Nereids – names of which the Egyptians had no knowledge, when Herodotus inquired. Those he believed to have been named by the Pelasgians,[151] with just one exception, Poseidon, whose name he claims to have Libyan origin. He makes it very clear in his text that he speak of the names of the gods as being imported, but is hesitant to say anything definite about the gods themselves:

---

[148] The division of *History* into nine books was not done by Herodotus.

[149] Herodotus, *History*, volume I, 2.49, translated by A. D. Godley, Loeb, London 1981, p.337.

[150] Herodotus, p.337.

[151] According to ancient Greek writers, the Pelasgians were people preceding the Hellenes in the Aegean area.

But whence each of the gods came in to being, or whether they had all for ever existed, and what outward forms they had, the Greeks knew not till (so to say) a very little while ago; for I suppose that the time of Hesiod and Homer was not more than four hundred years before my own; and these are they who taught the Greeks of the descent of the gods, and gave to all their several names, and honors and arts, and declared their outward forms.[152]

According to what he states earlier in his text, the deed of Homer and Hesiod was not that of the inventor, but of the messenger, since the names of the gods had already been given by the Egyptians. This Egyptian origin includes also the practices and rituals in connection with the gods:

the Greeks learnt all this from them. I hold this proved, because the Egyptian ceremonies are manifestly very ancient, and the Greek are of late origin.[153]

He certainly has a point – in his days Greek culture could still be measured in centuries, while the Egyptian civilization spanned millennia. Afore this, Herodotus expressed humble admiration in his book, not only in regard to the gods and their worship.

Classifying Herodotus is tricky. He treats the gods as foreign inventions, but refuses to call them fantasies. Still, it is not unlikely that he doubted their existence, altogether. He

[152] Herodotus, p.341.
[153] Herodotus, p.345.

may just have been reticent about it. On the other hand, it is also possible that he regarded the gods as real, although the initial knowledge of them was Egyptian and not Greek – that is, gods beyond national and cultural borders. Not to read too much into his statements, I classify his cosmology as polytheistic.

It should be added that the history of religion has proven him correct in general: substantial parts of Greek mythology are clearly influenced by older traditions of the region and its vicinities.

GORGIAS
Flourished 443 BC.

Although Gorgias (483-378 BC) has left us no particular thoughts on the gods and their myths, his three basic principles do not leave much room for any divinity – or anything else, for that matter: nothing exists, and if anything did exist, it could not be known to do so, and finally, if it could be known to exist, that knowledge could not be communicated. What could Gorgias be called, but the Nihilist?

There is drastic humor in his three propositions, as well as his arguments for them. According to the 2nd century CE philosopher Sextus Empiricus, Gorgias found that existence, or being, must have a beginning, or it would be unlimited and therefore nowhere. But if being began in being, it did not begin but already was. It could not have begun in not-being, because then not-being would have had to be some kind of being.

Gorgias took pride in rhetoric rather than sophism, wanting to teach the ability of persuasion, as Plato shows in the dialogue *Gorgias*. To the question from Socrates of what art he is skilled in, Gorgias bluntly replies: "Rhetoric, Socrates."[154] And he goes on to admit proudly that he is able to teach others the same – in essence: "the ability to persuade

---

[154] Plato, *Gorgias*, 449a, translated by W. R. M. Lamb, 1967, Perseus.

with speeches."[155] This power of persuasion was not obliged to hold the truth, but to make believable – something abominable to Socrates, as the unusual arrogance and harshness of his words in this dialogue indicate.

Yet, Gorgias' arguments against existence are not easily brushed aside, not even if applied to modern day big bang theory. In old Greece, his statement must have been a tremendous provocation to the pious. Another fragment of his reads:

> *Being is unrecognizable unless it succeeds in seeming,*
> *and seeming is weak unless it succeeds in being.*[156]

This again denies that something certain can be stated about anything. At the same time, if gods would seem to exist, although vaguely, it would be some kind of existence.

To Gorgias, there does not appear to be much of a distinction between what is and what might be. His unwillingness to adopt an ethic standpoint must have made good sense to him. When it is impossible to decide what is, how could one possibly claim the ability to judge it?

Since Gorgias believed in nothing at all, not even in the possibility of finding something out, his cosmology is most definitely an atheistic one. Gods might exist or not, but the truth about the matter is unreachable. To Gorgias, not even the gods themselves would be able to prove their existence.

---

[155] Plato, *Gorgias*, 452e.

[156] Freeman, Kathleen, *Ancilla to The Pre-Socratic Philosophers*, Oxford 1952, p.139.

MELISSUS
Flourished c. 442 BC.[157]

Melissus (Melissos, circa 482 BC-?) was the pupil of Parmenides. According to Diogenes Laertius, who has little to say about him, he was also in contact with Heraclitus.[158] This is highly unlikely, since Melissus was an infant at the time of Heraclitus' death. To Parmenides, the age difference was a little more than 30 years.

Melissus wrote one book, referred to with different titles in antiquity, one being *Concerning Nature or What Is*.[159]

According to Diogenes Laertius, Melissus said that we ought not to make any statements about the gods, because it is impossible to have knowledge of them.[160] Melissus regarded the universe as unlimited and forever the same, uniform, and completely full of matter. Any change or motion was only apparent, not real. Simplicius, the 6th century CE

---

[157] Diogenes Laertius says that Melissus flourished at the time of the 84th Olympiad, which was 444-441 BC. Diogenes Laertius, *Lives of Eminent Philosophers*, translated by R. D. Hicks, volume II, Loeb, London 1950, p.435.

[158] Diogenes Laertius, volume II, p.433. Diogenes' own dates for the flourishing of the philosophers sets them 60 years apart.

[159] Barnes, Jonathan, *The Presocratic Philosophers*, volume 1, London 1979, p.180.

[160] Diogenes Laertius, volume II, p.435.

philosopher whose writing contains all ten Melissus fragments remaining, quotes him saying:

> *That which was, was always and always will be. For if it had come into being, it necessarily follows that before it came into being, Nothing existed. If however Nothing existed, in no way could anything come into being out of nothing.*[161]

By the same method of reasoning he concluded that the world is one, uniform and unlimited, cannot move and cannot change.

Thereby, he would have to refuse the cosmogony given by Hesiod, and any portrayal of gods mighty enough to cause genuine change in the world – to add things or take things away, to disturb its uniformity or set it in motion. With such limitations, there would not be much divine remaining for the gods. Indeed, he makes no reference at all to them in his cosmology.

In stating that it is impossible to have any knowledge of the gods, Melissus may have masked a total disbelief in them. With this somewhat diplomatic thesis, he could hope to escape the fate of Protagoras, who was the same age as him. Protagoras had stated something similar about the gods, and was convicted of impiety for it. The tolerance of Greek society was limited, and it could be dangerous indeed to challenge.

[161] Freeman, Kathleen, *Ancilla to The Pre-Socratic Philosophers*, Oxford 1952, p.48.

Although it is not stated clearly in any of the fragments from him, atheism seems to be the only possible conclusion of Melissus' cosmology, so this is how I classify him.

Aphrodite teaches Eros to shoot. Bronze mirror cover, 4ᵗʰ century BC.

PROTAGORAS

Flourished c. 441 BC.

Most of those mentioned above had critical comments on how Homer and Hesiod portrayed the gods, but still insisted on their glorious existence, one way or another, or avoided exploring the issue. The sophist Protagoras (circa 481-411 BC) is said to have been driven out of Athens for doubting the very existence of the gods or, to be more precise, human ability to confirm it. His book *On the gods* (*Peritheon*) started with this statement:

> *As to the gods, I have no means of knowing either that they exist or that they do not exist. For many are the obstacles that impede knowledge, both the obscurity of the question and the shortness of human life.*[162]

For these words he was accused of impiety, resulting in his books being burned. According to some sources he was also expelled from Athens.[163] This fate of his shows that it

---

[162] Diogenes Laertius, *Lives of Eminent Philosophers*, translated by R. D. Hicks, volume II, Loeb, London 1950, p.465.

[163] Diogenes Laertius, volume II, p. 465. Among modern scholars there is some doubt about the trial and its consequences. Gagarin, Michael & Cohen, David, *The Cambridge Companion to Ancient Greek Law*, Cambridge 2005, p.66.

was not without risk to question the gods. There is a possibility that he had refrained from denying the existence of the gods completely, out of fear of judicial consequences – if so, a futile attempt.

His view on truth in general was that nothing is certain beyond the cognition of the individual mind, expressed in his famous saying:

> *Man is the measure of all things, of things that are that they are, and of things that are not that they are not.*[164]

The world is really what it is to the person perceiving it – though only to that one. To another person, the world is another. This principle, refuted by Plato in his dialogue *Theaetetus*,[165] makes it equally impossible to deny or confirm the existence of the gods – outside of the impression or conviction of the individual.

In the book Plato named after Protagoras, he and Socrates debate questions on virtue, its unity and adaptability.

---

[164] Diogenes Laertius, volume II, p. 463f.

[165] Plato has Socrates ridicule the thesis of Protagoras, by arguing that if what a man perceives as true is true, then if many regard this as untrue, it must be so – also to Protagoras, if he is to accept that what they perceive is true. Socrates admits that if Protagoras were present, he might have done a better job defending his thesis than Socrates and the others accomplish. Though he says so with little conviction, he would be more right than was his intention. Protagoras allows, in his thesis, for something to be true for one and untrue for another, not to say that it's the very substance of it. But to Plato the truth cannot be that impartial. Plato, *Theaetetus.*

They take turns in winning arguments, in a way that shows Plato's respect for Protagoras, although their fundamental views are irreconcilable. As sort of a peace offering, they digress into the analysis of an old poem by Simonides.[166]

Apart from the reaction to *On the gods*, Protagoras was uniquely successful as a lecturer for some 40 years, being able to charge as much as 100 minae for his lectures.[167] Plato says that he made more money than Phidias and ten other sculptors.

The burning of books must have been done thoroughly, and not restricted to *On the gods*. Only fragments remain of his writing, although it was voluminous. Diogenes Laertius makes him the pupil of Democritus,[168] but this is probably a mistake, considering that Protagoras was his senior with about 20 years.

Although it is likely that Protagoras had little faith in gods at all, he expressed himself so vaguely about the matter that I settle with classifying him as an agnostic.

[166] Plato, *Protagoras*.

[167] Diogenes Laertius, volume II, p.465. One talent equaled 60 minae, one mina equaled 100 drachmae. In the mid-5th century BC, a Mayor and a Member of Parliament received the daily pay of 1 drachma, which makes the fee of Protagoras unlikely. Moneymuseum.com.

[168] Diogenes Laertius, volume II, p. 463.

PHILOLAUS

Flourished c. 430 BC.

Philolaus of Croton (Philolaos, circa 470-385 BC) was a Pythagorean philosopher of distinction, although according to Diogenes Laertius he only wrote one book: *On Nature*. Diogenes writes unusually few words about this philosopher, but quotes the beginning of his only book:

> *Nature in the ordered universe was composed of unlimited and limiting elements, and so was the whole universe and all that is therein.*[169]

Regarding other philosophers, Diogenes often presents a long list of their writings, and quotes from them in a manner implying that he might very well have some of their texts in his library. With Philolaus, this is evidently not the case. Still, Diogenes stresses his importance, as the first one to write down the Pythagorean treatises, and the first one to state that the Earth moves in a circle. Diogenes also claims that the book by Philolaus influenced Plato's *Timaeus*, where cosmogony and cosmology are discussed.

---

[169] Diogenes Laertius, *Lives of Eminent Philosophers*, volume II, translated by R. D. Hicks, Cambridge Massachusetts 2005, p. 401.

Diogenes sums up the cosmology of Philolaus in a sentence:

His doctrine is that all things are brought about by necessity and in harmonious inter-relation.[170]

Aristotle surely had a copy of Philolaus' book, using it as a major source in presenting Pythagorean philosophy, which he did in *Metaphysics*. Plato mentions him in *Phaedo* and utilizes his metaphysics in *Philebus*.[171]

There is no indication of who might have been the teacher of Philolaus. If the estimated year of his birth is to be trusted, Pythagoras had been dead for up to 30 years, but there were other Pythagorean philosophers who might have introduced him to those ideas. He was far from only a Pythagorean, though. Neither Plato nor Meno, who was a pupil of Aristotle, mention him as such. His thoughts are likely to be responses to those of Anaxagoras and Parmenides.

His book is lost to us, and several of the fragments credited to him are definitely later forgeries, whereas others are generally regarded as authentic.

The cosmology of Philolaus differs significantly from that of most other philosophers of the pre-Socratic era. Where they see a universe ordered around the four elements air, water, fire and earth, or some of them, he divided the world order into unlimited things and limiting things. His

[170] Diogenes Laertius, volume II, p. 399.

[171] Huffman, Carl, Philolaus, *Stanford Encyclopedia of Philosophy*. plato.stanford.edu

definition of these two is not clear in the remaining fragments.

He argues that nothing more can be said for certain
about "nature in itself" and "the being of things", than that
the unlimited and the limiting must have been present for
the world to appear at all. Any additional understanding is
accessible to divine minds, but not to human ones. Yet, he is
convinced of how the world commenced:

> The first thing fitted together, the one in the center of the
> sphere, is called the hearth.[172]

That hearth is not the sun, but a central fire, around
which the sun orbits, as well as the stars, Earth and the
planets. The central fire, like everything else, is made up of
the unlimited and the limiting. In this case fire is the unlimited, whereas it is limited by its central position.

It is likely that by the unlimited Philolaus referred to
substance, and the limiting were shapes – matter brought to
some kind of order. For the unlimited and the limiting to
lead to the appearance of the world, they must be brought to
harmony, fitted together:

> Since these beginnings preexisted and were neither alike
> nor even related, it would not have been possible for them
> to be ordered, if a harmony had not come upon them.[173]

[172] Fragment 7. Huffman.
[173] Fragment 6. Huffman.

He describes this harmony with the musical scale of Pythagorean origin, the diatonic scale, where mathematical relations decide the tones of an octave. The same fixed ratios apply to the fitting together of the unlimited and the limiting.

There is no evidence of Philolaus agreeing or disagreeing with Pythagoras' theory of *metempsychosis*, the reincarnation of souls. What remains of his thoughts shows no signs of how he may have related to any kind of afterlife, nor do we know of his thoughts on the gods and their myths.

His cosmology shows no need of divine initiation or intervention, whatsoever. That is why I dare to classify it as atheistic. The universe of Philolaus is one of mathematical principles, just about as far from Homer and Hesiod as one can get.

LEUCIPPUS
Flourished c. 430 BC.

Regarding Leucippus (Leukippos, circa 470 BC-?) it is reasonable to do as Aristotle did in his writing, pairing him with his pupil Democritus. Almost nothing is known about his own life. He is said to have written only one book, *The Great World-Order*, the title implying that it would suffice. Yet, a remaining quotation is from a text entitled *On Mind*, which may be a chapter of it, or another book of his:

> *Nothing happens at random; everything happens out of reason and by necessity.*[174]

Leucippus and Democritus have the essence of their cosmology in common. Some basic terminology of it was probably invented by the former, though the latter is by far the most famous of the two, and more well-documented.

Diogenes Laertius says that Leucippus was a pupil to Zeno of Elea, and that he stated about the world:

> *The sum of things is unlimited, and they all change into one another. The all includes the empty as well as the*

[174]Freeman, Kathleen, *Ancilla to The Pre-Socratic Philosophers*, Oxford 1952, p.91.

full. The worlds are formed when atoms fall into the void and are entangled with one another; and from their motion as they increase in bulk arises the substance of the stars.[175]

The atom was to Leucippus a particle so small that it could not be divided. This concept was further developed by his pupil Democritus, but if Diogenes is to be trusted, much of the cosmology was formed already by Leucippus. This is also how Aristotle treats the two – as of one opinion in cosmological matters.[176]

The unlimited all, according to Leucippus, is made up of part full and part empty. To him, those are the real elements – full being the atoms, and empty being the space between them. Out of this mixture, numerous worlds arise and eventually dissolve. This happens through a vortex taking place when atoms enter the void. Thereby atoms that are alike join, arranging themselves according to their "shape, order and position"[177] into a spherical system. Also the Earth is formed out of this – into a drum-shape.

In line with the dynamics of the world as a whole, as well as any entity within it, birth is joining and death is dissolving. Also the soul, says Aristotle on Leucippus and his

[175] Diogenes Laertius, *Lives of Eminent Philosophers*, translated by R. D. Hicks, volume II, Loeb, London 1950, p.439ff.

[176] Aristotle, *Metaphysics*, 985b, translated by Hugh Lawson-Tancred, London 1998, p.17f.

[177] Aristotle, *Metaphysics*, p.18. Aristotle also uses the words 'shape, place and manner', as well as 'shape, arrangement and position', for the threesome.

disciple, is made of atoms. The atoms of the soul are rounded in shape, since such forms are the most freely movable, and the soul is what brings movement to the living creatures:

> *the spherical atoms are identified with soul because atoms of that shape are most adapted to permeate everywhere, and to set all the others moving by being themselves in movement. This implies the view that soul is identical with what produces movement in animals. That is why, further, they regard respiration as the characteristic mark of life.*[178]

In the atomic cosmos of Leucippus there is neither room nor any mission for gods. They are absent to the extent that he would have no need to deny their existence. The gods are so far away from his world-order that they might as well belong to a completely different universe. That makes the cosmology of Leucippus clearly atheistic.

The atomist cosmology of Leucippus and Democritus is commonly referred to as materialistic – a mechanical universe in no need of divine interference.

---

[178] Aristotle, *On the Soul*, 1.2, translated by J. A. Smith, classics.mit.edu.

DEMOCRITUS
Flourished c. 420 BC.

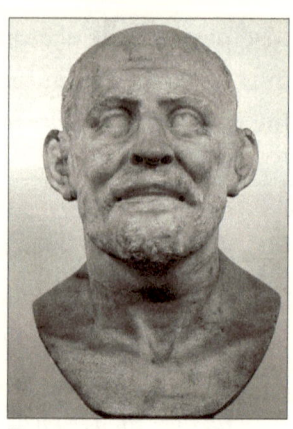

Democritus.

What Leucippus thought about cosmology and its atomic structure is generally assumed to be identical with the views of his pupil Democritus (Demokritos, circa 460-357 BC[179]), who elaborated further on the subject, being the one mostly quoted on it.

Diogenes Laertius gives a long list of books written by Democritus, dividing them into the groups ethics, virtue, physics, no head, mathematics, literature and music, and the arts. Most famous were *The Great Diacosmos* (world order) and *The Lesser Diacosmos*. Diogenes says that the former was by some attributed to Leucippus.[180]

---

[179] Though most of the Greek philosophers are reported to have had impressive life spans, these 103 years of Democritus can be questioned. His dates are quite uncertain. Hipparchus said 109 years, according to Diogenes Laertius, *Lives of Eminent Philosophers*, volume II, Loeb, 2005, p. 453. The historian Diodorus of Sicily, 1st century BC, says 90 in *The Library of History*, 14.11.5.

[180] Diogenes Laertius, volume II, p. 457.

Democritus made the theory of atoms the basis for all things in the world, including for example color as a difference in surface of the atoms, and taste as a difference in shape. According to Aristotle, he held a modest view toward learning: "Either there is no truth or it is concealed from us."[181] This may be a slight misinterpretation of his thoughts on perception:

> We know nothing accurately in reality, but (only) as it changes according to the bodily condition, and the constitution of those things that flow upon (the body) and impinge upon it.[182]

Since he held that all the senses work on an inflow of atoms carrying their respective characteristics, it was obvious to Democritus that one could not know reality as it was, but only as its fragments reached the observer. Regarding knowledge itself, he seems not to have been as modest as Aristotle has it.

Like his teacher Leucippus, Democritus did not involve the gods in his cosmos. So, although we have no statement of his swearing to it, at least in all cosmological matters he should be regarded as an atheist.

---

[181] Aristotle, *Metaphysics*, 1009b, translated by Hugh Lawson-Tancred, London 1998, p.100.

[182] Freeman, Kathleen, *Ancilla to The Pre-Socratic Philosophers*, Oxford 1952, p.93.

The Farnese Hercules. Roman copy by Glycon of a Greek Hellenistic original by Lysippus, c. 320 BC.

PRODICUS OF CEOS
Flourished c. 420 BC.

Prodicus (Prodikos, circa 460-395 BC) was a pupil of Protagoras and a well-paid sophist, not only by Plato implied to enjoy monetary gain. He was particularly interested in rhetoric and the careful choice of words. Prodicus was very popular, although he charged his pupils the steep fee of 50 drachmae.[183] Socrates, who had been to his lectures, joked about this:

> *Now if I had attended Prodicus's fifty drachma course of lectures, after which, as he himself says, a man has a complete education on this subject, there would be nothing to hinder your learning the truth about the correctness of names at once; but I have heard only the one drachma course, and so I do not know what the truth is about such matters.[184]*

---

[183] One talent equaled 60 minae, one mina equaled 100 drachmae. In the mid-5th century BC, a Mayor and a Member of Parliament received the daily pay of 1 drachma. Although steep, Prodicus' fee is more likely than that of Protagoras, who was said to earn as much as 100 minae for his lectures. Moneymuseum.com.

[184] Plato, *Cratylus*, 384b, translated by Harold N. Fowler 1921, Perseus.

Prodicus is not treated by Diogenes Laertius, and none of his writing remains. But his most famous work, *The Choice of Heracles*, is retold by Xenophon. When the mythical hero Heracles had left boyhood, he was at a solitary moment approached by two women:

> *The one was fair to see and of high bearing; and her limbs were adorned with purity, her eyes with modesty; sober was her figure, and her robe was white. The other was plump and soft, with high feeding. Her face was made up to heighten its natural white and pink, her figure to exaggerate her height. Open-eyed was she; and dressed so as to disclose all her charms. Now she eyed herself; anon looked whether any noticed her; and often stole a glance at her own shadow.*[185]

The first one was Joy, also called Virtue. The second – portrayed with so many more words – was Happiness, with the nickname Vice. Heracles had to choose between the two roads they showed him, that of Vice or that of Virtue, and the girls argued intensely for their respective merits. We need not wonder what choice the hero made.

More likely than his moral teaching, Prodicus' lack of belief in the divine could have provoked Athens, which was of limited tolerance. He is usually, among others by the 2nd century CE philosopher Sextus Empiricus, ranked as an atheist. That would help to explain the wide-spread inaccu-

---

[185] Xenophon, *Memorabilia*, 2.1.1, translated by O. J. Todd, Loeb, London 1979, p.95.

rate information about him being put to death for corrupting the youth of Athens. This is probably a confusion with the fate of Socrates, along with the alleged law of his homestead Ceos to have everyone over the age of sixty drink hemlock.[186] A similar mix-up may be the explanation to the words of Epicurean thought, incorrectly put in his mouth: "Where I am, death is not, and where death is, I am not."[187]

Regarding his atheism, the arguments are equally weak. In the remaining fragments of his own words, he has not spoken so categorically on the matter. What he clearly stated was that at least some gods were human inventions:

> *The ancients thought that sun and moon and rivers and springs, and in general everything that benefits the life of men were gods, because of the benefit coming from them.*[188]

Furthermore, according to the 4th century CE philosopher Themistius, Prodicus regarded all rites and cults as stemming from "the needs of farming", where he saw all kinds of piety have their beginning.[189] This was, of course, radical enough to earn him the hemlock, had the authorities sought him out.

---

[186] Freeman, Kathleen, *The Pre-Socratic Philosophers*, Oxford 1946, p.370.

[187] Freeman, p.374.

[188] Barnes, Jonathan, *The Presocratic Philosophers*, volume 2, London 1979, p.154.

[189] Barnes, p.156.

What is lacking in the above quotes is how he may have related to divinity as such. Denying the existence of some gods could not have been much less blasphemous than denying them all, but still creating a loophole in the event of being confronted. What gods the ancients created could be others than those worshiped by his contemporaries. Though the pious rituals may have commenced with farmers hoping to win the sympathy of higher powers, the powers in question could still have been as real and mighty as any priest would have them be.

Nevertheless, the sentiment of Prodicus points toward a serious doubt as to the existence of anything divine. That is why he is regarded as an atheist.

ANTISTHENES
Flourished c. 406 BC.

Antisthenes. Roman copy of a Greek marble original from around 300 BC.

Antisthenes (circa 446-366 BC), called the Cynic, was a pupil of Gorgias and then Socrates. He is often in the literature on myth mentioned as one to interpret the gods as personifications of natural forces. In the remainder of his works, though, there is little to support it.

He wrote about myths, and judging from the long list of his books in Diogenes Laertius, he did so repeatedly. But most of the titles suggest that he dealt with the ethics of living, the personal ideals suitable for man.

This includes texts on the legendary hero he seems to have pondered the most: Heracles, whose nobility, virtue and courage were like honey to Antisthenes. Personal virtue and stamina is also the subject in practically all of the quotes from him that Diogenes Laertius includes in his text, spanning several pages.[190]

---

[190] Diogenes Laertius, *Lives of Eminent Philosophers*, translated by R. D. Hicks, volume II, Loeb, London 1950, p.5ff.

Concerning the gods, ancient sources claim that Antisthenes made a distinction between the god of nature and the multitude of gods worshiped by men. Cicero complains:

> Antisthenes also, in his book entitled The Natural Philosopher, says that while there are many gods of popular belief, there is one god in nature, so depriving divinity of all meaning or substance.[191]

This view would, of course, give Antisthenes ambiguous feelings about the myths of Homer and Hesiod, but contains no indication of an allegorical interpretation of them.

The text usually referred to as evidence of Antisthenes' allegorical cosmology, is a passage in Xenophon's *Symposium* (3.5), regarding 'underlying meanings' (*hyponoiai*) in Homer's texts. This passage actually shows Socrates holding such views, whereas Antisthenes hardly seems to be familiar with the term.[192] His interest in the myths remains ethical, and his standpoint on the gods should be interpreted as monotheistic.

---

[191] Cicero, *De natura deorum*, 1.13.32, translated by H. Rackham, Loeb, London 1979, p.35.

[192] Rankin, H.D., *Antisthenes Sokratikos*, Amsterdam 1986, p.174.

DIAGORAS OF MELOS

Flourished c. 400 BC.

Not much is known about the poet and sophist Diagoras of Melos. He is not presented by Diogenes Laertius, and few fragments of his thoughts remain. For lack of any information on the matter, I estimate his year of flourishing to 400 BC, which should only be seen as an approximation. He was called atheist, not only in the meaning 'ungodly' of that word.

Athenagoras, a 2nd century CE philosopher who converted to Christianity, said about Diagoras that he "made the downright assertion that god does not exist at all."[193] Cicero states the same about him.[194]

Cicero also tells of how a friend of Diagoras tried to convince him of the existence of the gods. He pointed out that many votive pictures show people being saved from storms at sea by "dint of vows to the gods." Diagoras replied that "there are nowhere any pictures of those who have been shipwrecked and drowned at sea." And Cicero goes on to give another example, where Diagoras was on a ship in hard

---

[193] Barnes, Jonathan, *The Presocratic Philosophers*, volume 2, London 1979, p.151.

[194] Cicero, *De natura deorum*, 1.2, translated by H. Rackham, Loeb, London 1979, p.5.

weather, and the crew thought that they had brought it on themselves by taking this ungodly man on board. Diagoras asked them if the other boats out in the same storm also had a Diagoras on board.[195]

According to Sextus Empiricus he became an atheist when an enemy of his perjured himself in court and got away with it. In other sources there are some variations to this anecdote, though not changing its message: Immorality seems to go unpunished, so how can there be any gods in the sense of watchers over human virtue?

Diagoras is said to have been a pupil of Democritus, who may have initiated his disbelief in the existence of the gods. He was expelled from Athens in 411 BC for his attacks on religion.[196] Other sources claim that he was bought from slavery by Democritus in 411 BC, and then became his pupil.[197]

[195] Cicero, p.375.

[196] Freeman, Kathleen, *The Pre-Socratic Philosophers*, Oxford 1946, p.374.

[197] Freeman, p.292.

PLATO
Flourished 387 BC.

The head of an original bronze statue made by Sila-nion c. 350 BC.

The vast body of texts remaining from Plato (Platon, 427-347 BC) can not be thoroughly penetrated here, not even in regard to his views on the gods and the myths about them. On the other hand, a few of his dialogues treat this subject in particular. A closer look at them gives a good understanding of Plato's cosmology.

In *Timaeus*, the dialogue with Plato's most elaborate presentation of a cosmogony, he does not let his teacher Socrates speak on the subject, but the Pythagorean philosopher Timaeus, who has given the dialogue its name. He does so upon the request of Socrates, and to his liking.

Timaeus starts by stating his opinion on a matter having been discussed by most of the philosophers – whether the world is created or not, eternal or with a beginning and thereby a possible end. The former would only be perceived by reason, the latter only by the senses. Timaeus concludes about the world:

It has come into existence; for it is visible and tangible and possessed of a body; and all such things are sensible.[198]

For something to come into existence there must be a cause, and that cause is the creator, an eternal being of perfection. This is the *demiurge*, the craftsman, the maker of the world, far from a god in the sense of the Greek mythology. The demiurge wanted to make an image of his perfection, a finite impression of the infinite. His reason for this was as pure and noble as his being:

He was good, and in him that is good no envy ariseth ever concerning anything; and being devoid of envy He desired that all should be, so far as possible, like unto Himself.[199]

There is a striking resemblance between the creator of Timaeus and the biblical one, except for the significant fact that to the former it is the whole world which will be an image of its creator, instead of, as in the latter, man. Man is, to Timaeus, far from enough of a model to carry any likeness to the world creator. Only the whole will do. To have any likeness to its creator, and to excel in beauty, it must be endowed with reason and a soul.

But the world was not created out of nothingness. To the minds of the Greeks, the making of something out of noth-

---

[198] Plato, *Timaeus*, 28b-c, translated by W. R. M. Lamb, 1925, Perseus.

[199] Plato, *Timaeus*, 29e.

ing, *creatio ex nihilo*, would be absurd. The benevolent creator had something to work on:

> *He took over all that was visible, seeing that it was not in a state of rest but in a state of discordant and disorderly motion, He brought it into order out of disorder.*[200]

There was something in the world before the act of creation, a disorder, put into order by the creator. That was the nature of creation – giving a divinely beautiful order to the primordial chaos. This order was based on proportion. The parts were balanced with each other, a divine symmetry often expressed by mathematics.

An original pair was constructed out of necessity: "without fire nothing could ever become visible, nor tangible without some solidity, nor solid without earth."[201] Thus, the two elements fire and earth were born, but proportion demanded that they were accompanied by two more: air and water. As for the shape of the whole world, there was only one possibility:

> *Now for that Living Creature which is designed to embrace within itself all living creatures the fitting shape will be that which comprises within itself all the shapes there are; wherefore He wrought it into a round, in the shape of a sphere, equidistant in all directions from the*

---

[200] Plato, *Timaeus*, 30a.
[201] Plato, *Timaeus*, 31b.

center to the extremities, which of all shapes is the most perfect and the most self-similar.[202]

He allowed for it only one motion: a rotation within itself, belonging in particular to reason and intelligence. And this world god – the term god is used on this creation – was made to need no other but itself, all in all "a blessed God."[203] Its soul was mixed in a complex fashion out of three substances: the Same, the Other and Being.

For the eternal being, there is neither past nor future, it just is, but for a world with a starting point there was need for time, which was created simultaneously with the world, so that the one would not survive the other. Thereby the problem regarding what was before creation got solved: There was no time before creation, therefore nothing can have existed before it, not even a nothing.[204]

For the purpose of being recorders of the passing of time, the heavenly bodies were created – the sun and moon, as well as the planets, given their respective orbs. Timaeus must confess that, though the periods marked by the cycles of the sun and moon are easy enough to understand, the chronology that the planets mark is yet to be deciphered by man. A time span of utter significance is that, when all the planets

[202] Plato, *Timaeus*, 33b.

[203] Plato, *Timaeus*, 34b.

[204] S:t Augustine (354-430 CE) had a similar explanation, stating that God created time by starting movement in the universe. Modern big bang theory supposes the same: time exists within the universe, and neither outside nor before it.

have returned to a constellation they had before, and the whole process starts anew:

> the complete number of Time fulfils the Complete Year when all the eight circuits, with their relative speeds, finish together and come to a head, when measured by the revolution of the Same and Similarly-moving.[205]

This, the Great World-Year, a concept familiar to the Greek as well as earlier astrological traditions, Plato seems to have estimated to 36,000 years[206] – not by any astronomical calculations.

Again for reasons of proportion and symmetry, the number of kinds of living creatures should equal that of the elements: gods for fire, birds for air, fish for water and land walking creatures for earth.

The gods were made round, like the shape of the world itself, and they were the fixed stars. Timaeus does not name them, but to the Greeks the stars in question were no mystery. Regarding the gods known through the mythology of Homer and Hesiod, Timaeus suddenly speaks with a diplomatic humility, reeking with irony:

> Concerning the other divinities, to discover and declare their origin is too great a task for us, and we must trust to those who have declared it aforetime, they being, as

---

[205] Plato, *Timaeus*, 39d.

[206] Plato, *Republic*, 546b, translated by Paul Shorey, 1969, Perseus.

*they affirmed, descendants of gods and knowing well, no
doubt, their own forefathers.*[207]

It is hard not to interpret this comment as expressing a
doubt in the existence of all those lesser gods, among which
he counts such dignities as Uranus, Cronos, Hera, and even
Zeus himself.

The creator of the world addressed the gods, explaining
to them that they be immortal – although not indestructible.
For the creation of mortals it would be necessary that those
would not have the same high creator as the immortals:

*But if by my doing these creatures came into existence
and partook of life, they would be made equal unto
gods.*[208]

Therefore, he left it up to the gods to create the beings of
air, water and earth. But the souls of those lesser beings, the
high creator took upon himself. He used the same mixture as
for the soul of the world, by this time far less pure, especially
after again being mixed. This potion was split into as many
parts as the stars in the sky, one given to each of them. Now,
these star souls were to be born in the flesh of men. If living
righteously, they would get to return to their star, otherwise
they would be reborn in lesser bodies, until learning to live
justly – by having their reason control their emotions.

---

[207] Plato, *Timaeus*, 40d.

[208] Plato, *Timaeus*, 41c.

In his dialogue *Gorgias*, Plato speaks differently about the soul's adventures after death. Here he refers to the gods of Homer, starting his tale with the remark:

Give ear then, as they say, to a right fine story, which you will regard as a fable, I fancy, but I as an actual account; for what I am about to tell you I mean to offer as the truth.[209]

It should be noted that he takes for granted that such a tale of gods in the heavens would not be taken seriously. So, it is likely that the truth contained therein is allegorical.

He explains that righteous men were sent to the Isles of the Blessed, whereas the villains went to "the dungeon of requital and penance which, you know, they call Tartarus."[210] But in the distant times where those proceedings started, this judgement was passed on people at the end of their lives, so their judges were influenced by their outer appearances. Zeus decided that they should be judged after death, when bodies and souls were separated from each other, naked and completely revealed. People also had to be ignorant of the time of their death, so that they would be unprepared. And more was needed:

Their judge also must be naked, dead, beholding with very soul the very soul of each.[211]

---

[209] Plato, *Gorgias*, 523a, translated by W. R. M. Lamb, 1967, Perseus.

[210] Plato, *Gorgias*, 523b.

[211] Plato, *Gorgias*, 523e.

That separation, explains Socrates, is what death really is:

death, as it seems to me, is actually nothing but the disconnection of two things, the soul and the body, from each other.[212]

They both keep their traits and characters. The soul of the vicious is punished, as a warning to others and to repent. The worst sinners will forever remain, but those of minor fault will eventually be benefitted thereby.

The majority of the incorrigible ones are rulers, Socrates states: "most of those in power, my excellent friend, prove to be bad." On the other hand, in the rare case of a mighty man living righteously, there is cause for praise.[213] Socrates evidently doubted that there would be many with the freedom of choice, who would refrain from using it viciously.

In *Phaedrus* the soul is spoken of in a mythical type of metaphor, which is interesting as an example of how Plato allowed himself to use the symbols of mythology:

We will liken the soul to the composite nature of a pair of winged horses and a charioteer. Now the horses and charioteers of the gods are all good and of good descent, but those of other races are mixed; and first the charioteer of the human soul drives a pair, and secondly one of the

[212] Plato, *Gorgias*, 524b.
[213] Plato, *Gorgias*, 526a.

horses is noble and of noble breed, but the other quite the
opposite in breed and character. Therefore in our case the
driving is necessarily difficult and troublesome.[214]

When it comes to the myths, Plato presents an ambiguous standpoint. He is not above inventing some little myth to promote good behavior in the citizens, a "noble lie", letting Socrates suggest for that purpose:

something that has happened ere now in many parts of
the world, as the poets aver and have induced men to be-
lieve, but that has not happened and perhaps would not
be likely to happen in our day and demanding no little
persuasion to make it believable.[215]

Anyway, he insists that there is some truth to be found in myth:

we begin by telling children fables, and the fable is, taken
as a whole, false, but there is truth in it also.[216]

In consideration of these tales being taught to children in bad need of proper directions, Plato expresses the necessity of censorship. Among the many unhealthy fables, Socrates mentions those of Hesiod and Homer:

---

[214] Plato, *Phaedrus*, 246a-b, translated by Harold N. Fowler, 1925, Perseus.

[215] Plato, *Republic*, 414b-c.

[216] Plato, *Republic*, 377a.

*These, methinks, composed false stories which they told
and still tell to mankind.*[217]

The greatest lie is what Hesiod said about the bestialities
done by Uranus and Cronus to one another, then by the son
of Cronus unto him. In the myth, Cronus castrated his father
Uranus. The son of Cronus was Zeus, who defeated him at
war. Socrates complains:

*Even if they were true I should not think that they ought
to be thus lightly told to thoughtless young persons.*[218]

In the dialogue *Cratylus*, the question of names and what
the names stand for is ventilated in a way that borders to
parody, then again seems serious enough. What gods there
can be behind their names, and if there are such things as
true names as well as false ones, is pondered with numerous
examples – some more probable than others. In the midst of
his joking comments, Socrates applies the analysis of names
as bearers of character or fate, to that of Zeus, whose name
he thinks has "an excellent meaning, although hard to be
understood." This divine name is made up of two, he
explains:

*for some call him Zena, and use the one half, and others
who use the other half call him Dia; the two together
signify the nature of the God, and the business of a name,*

217 Plato, *Republic*, 377d.
218 Plato, *Republic*, 378a.

as we were saying, is to express the nature. For there is
none who is more the author of life to us and to all, than
the lord and king of all. Wherefore we are right in calling
him Zena and Dia, which are one name, although di-
vided, meaning the God through whom all creatures al-
ways have life (di on zen aei pasi tois zosin uparchei).[219]

He goes on to analyze in a similar manner the names of
Cronus and Uranus, as well as many other gods and heavenly bodies. In the name of the moon (*selene*) he finds the
indication that it receives its light from the sun, though it
should then more correctly be called *selaenoneoaeia*. He also
gives an explanation to the very term god (*theos*):

I suspect that the sun, moon, earth, stars, and heaven,
which are still the Gods of many barbarians, were the
only Gods known to the aboriginal Hellenes. Seeing that
they were always moving and running, from their
running nature they were called Gods or runners
(Theous, Theontas); and when men became acquainted
with the other Gods, they proceeded to apply the same
name to them all.[220]

Yet, he insists that names are only imitations of what
they link to. At best they can be made up by intelligent
minds to teach people important things, by way of their
meanings. But names are not to be trusted unconditionally,

[219] Plato, *Cratylus*, translated by Benjamin Jowett, 1892, Gutenberg.

[220] Plato, *Cratylus*.

by whatever method of analysis. Socrates ends by saying to Cratylus:

> *Reflect well and like a man, and do not easily accept such a doctrine; for you are young and of an age to learn. And when you have found the truth, come and tell me.*[221]

Certainly, Socrates drank the poison before that day.

In Plato's mind, as it reveals itself through the dialogues, there is not much trust in the gods of Homer and Hesiod. Plato's cosmology is two-layered: a polytheism, and beyond it the monotheism of the demiurge. Since the gods of the polytheistic layer are nothing but artefacts and servants of the demiurge, who is alone in being eternal and in creating the world, it makes the most sense to classify Plato's cosmology as monotheistic – somewhat monotheistic.

---

[221] Plato, *Cratylus.*

ARISTOTLE
Flourished 344 BC.

Aristotle. Roman marble copy of a Greek original from the last quarter of the 4th century BC, with the nose restored.

From Aristotle (Aristoteles, 384-322 BC), just as with his teacher Plato, a mass of writing remains. Luckily, regarding myths and things of divine nature, Aristotle makes the task easier than does Plato. One of his books is particularly concentrated on the subject: *Metaphysics*. Here he gives a personally commented, often critical review of past theories of cosmology, and presents his own. For a sufficient coverage of his perspectives on these matters, *Metaphysics* will do.

His judgement on myth can be harsh, as expressed in comments on "the school of Hesiod" and similar "theologians". They have said that those who do not eat the nectar and ambrosia are mortal, but Aristotle questions how immortals can be of need of food. Then he plainly states:

*about those who have invented clever mythologies it is
not worthwhile to take a serious look.*[222]

On the other hand, he also speaks very appreciatively
about the myths: Lovers of stories are in a way lovers of
wisdom, since stories were composed of wonders that make
man start to philosophize. Those wonders are mainly astronomical and cosmological ones.[223]

His favorable attitude to myth is also evident in *The
Poetics,* his book on the mechanics of drama and storytelling.
There, he praises Homer repeatedly for being so skilled in
composing good stories. Aristotle regards the main function
of drama to be *catharsis,* an emotional release for the specta-
tors.[224] Myths, when acted out or retold, would have the
same function.

Aristotle describes the birth of mythology in close detail,
in connection to his discussion on how many primal movers
and movements there can be. He is referring to the multitude
of gods. Tradition needs to be considered:

> *From old – and indeed extremely ancient – times there
> has been handed down to our later age intimations of a
> mythical character to the effect that the stars are gods and
> that the divine embraces the whole of nature. The further
> details were subsequently added in the manner of myth.*

[222] Aristotle, *Metaphysics,* 1000a, translated by Hugh Lawson-Tancred, London 1998, p.68f.

[223] Aristotle, *Metaphysics,* p.9.

[224] Aristotle, *Poetics,* translated by Stephen Halliwell, Loeb, London 1999.

*Their purpose was the persuasion of the masses and gen-
eral legislative and political expediency. For instance, the
myths tell us that these gods are anthropomorphic or
resemble some of the other animals and give us other,
comparable extrapolations of the basic picture.*[225]

Aristotle suggests that the embroidered details should be
discarded, to recognize that in mythical perspectives the
primary substances were gods. He also points out that although many other arts and doctrines may have perished
through time:

*these ancient cosmologies have been preserved, like holy
relics, right up to the present day.*[226]

His own supreme deity is the primal mover of the universe, who set things in motion. This is someone so elevated
as to be only thinking – the highest form of life – and thinking about thinking, at that. In this tautological fashion, the
supreme being is untarnished, untouchable, closed within its
own perfection. Were it to think about anything other than
its own thinking, it would be vulnerable, in risk of losing its
grandeur or its perfection. He calls this being god, and makes
this definition:

[225] Aristotle, *Metaphysics*, p.380.
[226] Aristotle, *Metaphysics*, p.380f.

God is a supreme and eternal living being, so that to God belong life and continuous and eternal duration. For that is what God is.[227]

Aristotle's cosmology is more clear and doubtless in its monotheism than that of his teacher Plato, who seems unwilling to give up the multitude of Greek gods completely. Aristotle's primal mover is as elevated from the world as is Plato's *demiurge*, but in addition, his world is all in all a worldly place. There are no gods allowed exceptions from the natural laws of it. The only thing divine in Aristotle's universe is the initiator of it.

[227] Aristotle, *Metaphysics*, p.374.

EPICURUS
Flourished 301 BC.

Epicurus. Marble copy of a Greek bronze original from early 3ʳᵈ century BC.

Epicurus (Epikuros, 341-270 BC) had two principal teachers – the Platonist Pamphilus in his teens, and Nausiphanes of Teos, who introduced him to the atomism of Democritus, in his twenties. But he distanced himself from both of them firmly, calling the latter a scoundrel, to form his own school of thought, which was extraordinary in allowing both sexes as pupils.[228]

The principal source to his life and theories is Diogenes Laertius, who wrote appreciatively and extensively about him in *Lives of Eminent Philosophers*. Epicurus is said to have written some 300 books, but what remains is principally some letters of his, and fragments mostly in the form of aphorisms.[229] Among the letters, there is one known as the *Lesser Epitome*, written to his pupil Herodotus, later to break with and loudly criticize him. This letter lays out the general

[228] O'Connor, Eugene, *The Essential Epicurus*, New York 1993, p.9ff.

[229] O'Connor, p.12.

lines of his cosmology as well as his ethics. Letters to some other pupils also remain, confirming the philosophy of Epicurus.

He stated that since nothing can be created from what does not exist, the universe must always have existed and always will. It consists of space and bodies made up of atoms, in continual motion. The universe must also be unlimited, since there cannot be a nothing outside of it. But within it is a multitude of worlds:

> there is an infinite number of worlds, some like this world, others unlike it.[230]

These worlds are created out of the infinite, and then dissolved, some sooner and some later.

Regarding the soul, Epicurus is quite precise:

> the soul is a corporeal thing, composed of fine particles, dispersed all over the frame, most nearly resembling wind with an admixture of heat, in some respects like wind, in others like heat. But again, there is the third part which exceeds the other two in the fineness of its particles and thereby keeps in closer touch with the rest of the frame.[231]

---

[230] Diogenes Laertius, *Lives of Eminent Philosophers*, translated by R. D. Hicks, volume II, Loeb, London 1950, p.575.

[231] Diogenes Laertius, volume II, p.595.

The body is unable to sense anything without the soul, as is the soul without the body. Therefore, when the soul leaves the body, no awareness remains. According to Epicurus, there cannot be any afterlife. Death is a complete stop. This he regards as a reason not to worry at all about dying:

> death is nothing to us, for good and evil imply sentience,
> and death is the privation of all sentience.[232]

Life can only be enjoyable if one ceases to yearn for immortality, and renounces the fear of an endless afterlife in one or other torment:

> either because of the myths, or because we are in dread of
> the mere insensibility of death, as if it had to do with
> us.[233]

When dying is simply ceasing to perceive, to feel, to be, there is nothing in it to dread.

> Death, therefore, the most awful of evils, is nothing to us,
> seeing that, when we are, death is not come, and, when
> death is come, we are not.[234]

Therefore, learning to live well is not different from learning to die well. The only reasonable way to prepare for

---

[232] Diogenes Laertius, volume II, p.651.

[233] Diogenes Laertius, volume II, p.611.

[234] Diogenes Laertius, volume II, p.651.

the latter is to do the former the fullest one can, in itself and for itself.

It is when theorizing about celestial perspectives that Epicurus gives his views on the gods. The dynamics of the heavens, such as planetary movements, eclipses and so forth, take place:

> *without the ministration or command, either now or in the future, of any being who at the same time enjoys perfect bliss along with immortality.*[235]

He has a slightly humorous way of robbing the gods of their powers by complimenting them, stating that such blissful creatures could not be dealing with troublesome worldly matters, or they would not be so blissful. They are above the world. It is implied but not outspoken by Epicurus that they are also completely without role in or relevance to existence:

> *the divine nature must not on any account be adduced to explain this, but must be kept free from the task and in perfect bliss.*[236]

It is as much saying that they do not exist at all, as is possible without actually saying it. So he dares to continue by stating that misconceptions on this matter are chief frustrations to man:

[235] Diogenes Laertius, volume II, p.607.
[236] Diogenes Laertius, volume II, p.625.

the greatest anxiety of the human mind arises through
the belief that the heavenly bodies are blessed and inde-
structible, and that at the same time they have volitions
and actions and causality inconsistent with this belief.[237]

What can be said about the cosmos, he stresses repeatedly, is only that which can be perceived about it. Therefore,
in many cases, not much at all can be confirmed exclusively.
More often than not, there are several possibilities, such as
with the question of the size of heavenly bodies:

The size of the sun and the remaining stars relatively to
us is just as great as it appears. But in itself and actually
it may be a little larger or a little smaller, or precisely as
great as it is seen to be.[238]

What he strongly objects to is stating one theory to be
true and not the other, although there is no actual proof of it:

But one must not be so much in love with the explana-
tion by a single way as wrongly to reject all the others
from ignorance of what can, and what cannot, be within
human knowledge, and consequent longing to discover
the indiscoverable.[239]

Both mythology and philosophy can be blamed for this.

[237] Diogenes Laertius, volume II, p.611.

[238] Diogenes Laertius, volume II, p.619.

[239] Diogenes Laertius, volume II, p.623.

Epicurus does not clearly state an atheistic conviction in the fragments of his words that remain. It is easy to see that his cosmology has little need of gods to perform any of its functions. Consequently, it is hard to see what room there would at all be for gods in his world. In other words: There is no concrete evidence of him being an atheist, but it would be extremely difficult to argue for classifying him as anything else.

ZENO OF CITIUM
Flourished 293 BC.

Zeno of Citium.

Stoic philosophy was founded by Zeno (Zenon, 333-261 BC), pupil of Crates. None of his own writing remains, and the spread of Stoicism should rather be credited to the work and extensive writing of Chrysippus (c.282-206 BC). Regarding cosmology and the divine, the Stoics essentially share the same view, so Zeno is as good a representative as any other in Hellenic Greece.

This is also the choice of Diogenes Laertius, the main source to the thoughts of Zeno and several other Stoic philosophers. He chooses to present Stoic philosophy in his extensive chapter on Zeno, because he was the founder of it.[240]

The Stoics divided their philosophical doctrine into three parts – logical, physical and ethical.[241] Their physical philosophy, dealing with cosmology and the inner workings of the world, is the one relevant to the subject of this book. But to them their logics and physics were paving the way for their

---

[240] Diogenes Laertius, *Lives of Eminent Philosophers*, translated by R. D. Hicks, volume II, Loeb, London 1950, 149.

[241] Diogenes Laertius, volume II, 149.

ethics, their ideas of virtue as opposed to vice, and the recommendable way to live one's life.

Stoic cosmology saw the whole world as one living being, with one soul. This soul they could call god, but it is very different from the divine beings portrayed by Homer and Hesiod. It is the reason and intentional mind of the world. God is one word for it, others are Reason, Fate, or Zeus.

In the beginning, this eternal and indestructible being was by itself, creating the world by a transformation through the four elements fire, air, water and earth, in that order. They arranged themselves from outer to inner, in a spherical shape of the universe, with the Earth at the center.[242] This creation process is repeated at long intervals, by the creator absorbing all substance and then emitting it again.

The souls of men are parts of the world soul. A virtuous man should simply accept the order given by the world, and the events appearing. In Zeno's words:

life in agreement with nature.[243]

There was little or no room for free will in the Stoic universe, a monotheistic cosmology taken to the extreme: the world and its population being nothing but parts of its creator.

---

[242] Diogenes Laertius, volume II, 241.

[243] Diogenes Laertius, volume II, 195.

EUHEMERUS
Flourished c. 290 BC.

Although the historian Euhemerus (Euhemeros, circa 330-260 BC) never made himself a name comparable in grandeur to that of the majority above, he hung on to posterity by his very name. Theory on myth and religion along his line of thought is called *euhemerism*.

He saw myth as history in disguise, where the gods being worshiped were originally living men. They had been elated in this way because of some great feat of theirs, or their shiny virtue, perhaps sometimes simply because of all the power they had when alive. Men who had been glorified when alive, had by later generations been deified.

This theory was adopted and applied by numerous scholars during all of the Christian era, well into our days, more or less similarly to how its originator had used it.

The most elaborate presentation of Euhemerus is by Diodorus of Sicily in *The Library of History*, from the 1st century BC, when discussing what different theories the ancients had regarding the gods:

> *Certain of the gods, they say, are eternal and imperishable, such as the sun and the moon and the other stars of the heavens, and the winds as well and whatever else possesses a nature similar to theirs; for of each of these*

the genesis and duration are from everlasting to everlasting. But the other gods, we are told, were terrestrial beings who attained to immortal honor and fame because of their benefactions to mankind, such as Heracles, Dionysus, Aristaeus, and the others who were like them. Regarding these terrestrial gods many and varying accounts have been handed down by the writers of history and of mythology; of the historians, Euhemerus, who composed the Sacred History, has written a special treatise about them, while, of the writers of myths, Homer and Hesiod and Orpheus and the others of their kind have invented rather monstrous stories about the gods.[244]

Diodorus goes on to present Euhemerus as a friend of king Cassander, first ruler of Macedonia after the death of Alexander, himself to remain on the throne no more than four years until his death. It was Cassander who sent Euhemerus to sea on international errands, going southward from Arabia for a number of days, before carried to shore on the island of Panchaea.

On this island he saw pious inhabitants worship their gods with magnificent sacrifices. He found a temple to Zeus, in which there were written the deeds of Uranus, Cronus and Zeus – when they were men who walked the Earth.

Euhemerus goes on to say that Uranus was the first to be king, that he was an honorable man and beneficent, who

[244] Diodorus of Sicily, *The Library of History*, book VI, translated by C. H. Oldfather, volume 3, Cambridge 1970, p.331.

was versed in the movement of the stars, and that he was also the first to honor the gods of the heavens with sacrifices, whence he was called Uranus, or "Heaven". There were born to him by his wife Hestia two sons, Titan and Cronus, and two daughters, Rhea and Demeter. Cronus became king after Uranus, and marrying Rhea he begat Zeus and Hera and Poseidon. And Zeus, on succeeding to the kingship, married Hera and Demeter and Themis, and by them he had children, the Curetes by the first named, Persephone by the second, and Athena by the third. And going to Babylon he was entertained by Belus, and after that he went to the island of Panchaea, which lies in the ocean, and here he set up an altar to Uranus, the founder of his family.[245]

Thus, the whole Olympian community began as a human family matter. Euhemerus further tells of Zeus conquering Cilicia and visiting many other nations:

all of which paid honor to him and publicly proclaimed him a god.[246]

It is generally assumed that the island of Panchea, as well as the rest of what Euhemerus tells, is more or less fiction of his. Yet, this approach to mythology, seeing behind it some distant historical facts, did not lose its credibility. Myths, also those involving the gods, even the very genesis

---

[245] Diodorus of Sicily, p.335.

[246] Diodorus of Sicily, p. 335.

of them as well as the whole world, tend to be mingled with the affairs of men. In this, Homer is certainly a good example, having gods and men interact to the extent that they become difficult to tell apart at all.

To the Christian thinkers, the ideas of Euhemerus had the additional advantage of doing away with the heathen ingredient in the Greek myths, without having to do away with the myths altogether. The stories of old could be nourished and retold, with an interpretation doing pretty much the reverse of what Euhemerus said once had taken place: Men having been turned into gods could be turned back into men.

Since Euhemerus claimed that the highest of the gods, even Zeus himself, had been men, there could not have been much of a divine sphere left for him to believe in. What could he have been but an atheist, at least as far as the Greek gods are concerned? Yet, we have no clear statement of this from him, nor do we know what kind of cosmology he supported. His important contribution is that of his historical explanation to myth, so that is how to classify him.

APPENDIX

Marble gravestone sphinx, from about 550 BC.

SCHOOLS OF GREEK PHILOSOPHY

Traditionally, the Greek philosophers are grouped according to philosophical schools. This is easier to find with some than with others, and that can be said also about the meaningfulness of it. Here are two lists of philosophers, sorted according to the schools. The first one is from Diogenes Laertius, and the second one is my compilation, based on what is common among present day scholars.

Several of the philosophers on the lists are not treated in this book.

Diogenes Laertius makes a simple and straightforward division into two groups, based on geographic roots. One is Ionian, commenced by Thales, the other Italian, with Pherecydes as its originator. He then lists the philosophers chronologically in each group. In the Ionian group he divides the followers of Socrates into three lines. None of the philosophers on this list lived later than the 2nd century BC.[247]

Greek philosophers according to Diogenes Laertuius
Ionian
Thales
Anaximander
Anaximenes
Anaxagoras
Archelaus
Socrates

Plato	Antisthenes	(Plato)
Speusippus	Diogenes the Cynic	Aristotle
Xenocrates	Crates of Thebes	Theophrastus

[247] Diogenes Laertius, *Lives of Eminent Philosophers*, translated by R. D. Hicks, volume I, Loeb, London 1995, 15ff.

Polemo	Zeno of Citium
Crantor	Cleanthes
Crates	Chrysippus
Arcesilaus	
Lacydes	
Carneades	
Clitomachus	

Italian
Pherecydes
Pythagoras
Telauges
Xenophanes
Parmenides
Zeno of Elea
Leucippus
Democritus
Nausiphanes (and Naucydes)
Epicurus

Diogenes also suggests that the philosophers can be divided into dogmatists and sceptics. The former claim that something can be asserted about things, the latter that things are unknowable. He makes no list based on those groups. Furthermore, he mentions the many schools and how they got their names, but again without listing the philosophers belonging to them.[248]

To a large extent, the grouping done by Diogenes is still used. Contrary to his situation, though, our material on Greek philosophers is completely dominated by the writings

---

[248] Diogenes Laertius, 17ff.

of two of them – Plato and Aristotle. Of their predecessors, little more than fragments remain.

Therefore, it has become meaningful to make the distinction *pre-Socratics*, for all those who were his seniors. They reach us almost exclusively through secondary sources. It is also common to adapt the *Hellenistic* period used for Greece after the death of Alexander, in 323 BC. This is suitable in philosophy, since it differs only one year from the death of Aristotle, in 322 BC.

This leads to three periods:

Pre-Socratic, in the 6th and 5th century BC
Socratic, in the 4th century BC
Hellenistic, in the 3rd and 2nd century BC

The schools of Greek philosophy continued longer, but with almost none of the significance they had during those first few centuries. Plato's Academy was not closed until 529 CE, by Emperor Justinian, but had not produced any mind even remotely close to the importance of its founder.

Aristotle's Lyceum was sacked by the Roman General Lucius Cornelius Sulla in 86 BC, but reconstructed some time after that. Still, its continued days were so anonymous that we have no knowledge of when the school ceased to exist.

As for the Greek schools of philosophy, a modern grouping of the philosophers can be done in the following way, without much controversy.

Schools of Greek Philosophy
Pre-Socratic period

Ionians
  Milesian
    Thales , Anaximander, Anaximenes
  Xenophanes
  Ephesian
    Heraclitus, Cratylus
  Diogenes of Apollonia

Italian
  Pherecydes
  Pythagoreans
    Pythagoras, Alcmaeon, Philolaus, Archytas, Timaeus
  Eleatics
    Parmenides, Melissus, Zeno of Elea
Pluralists
  Empedocles, Anaxagoras
  Atomists
    Leucippus, Democritus
Sophists
  Protagoras, Gorgias, Hippias, Prodicus, Thrasymachus, Antiphon

Socratic period
Socrates
Xenophon
Plato
  Speusippus, Xenocrates
  Aristotle
    Peripatetics
      Theophrastus, Aristoxenus, Eudemus, Clearchus, Strato
    Megarians
      Euclides, Eubulides, Stilpo, Diodorus Cronus

Cynics
> Antisthenes, Diogenes of Sinope

Cyrenaics
> Aristippus of Cyrene

Hellenistic period
Sceptics
> Pyrrho, Timon, Arcesilaus, Carneades, Aenesidemus

Cynics
> Crates of Thebes, Menippus

Stoics
> Zeno of Citium, Aristo, Cleanthes, Chrysippus, Antipater,
> Crates of Mallus

Epicureans
> Epicurus, Hermarchus

LIST OF GREEK PHILOSOPHERS

The list below is not complete, but all the significant Greek philosophers of the era are listed, as well as some who must be regarded as peripheral and others who are called historians rather than philosophers. No philosopher who lived in the Christian Era is included.

They are listed in alphabetical order. The dates of their birth and death are rarely certain, sometimes completely unknown and therefore only estimated. Those estimates are generally accepted (although sometimes differing a few years between sources). Where no established estimate exists, there is a question mark.

Greek Philosophers BCE

Aenesidemus (1st century BC)
Alcmaeon (5th century BC)
Anaxagoras (500-428 BC)
Anaximander (610-546 BC)
Anaximenes (585-528 BC)
Antipater of Tarsus (144-? BC)
Antiphon (480-411 BC)
Antisthenes (446-366 BC)
Arcesilaus (316-232 BC)
Archytas (428-347 BC)
Aristippus of Cyrene (435-356 BC)
Aristo of Chios (290-? BC)
Aristotle (384-322 BC)
Aristoxenus (4th century BC)
Chrysippus (280-207 BC)
Cleanthes (331-232 BC)
Clearchus (4th century BC)
Crates of Mallus (2nd century BC)
Crates of Thebes (368-288 BC)

Cratylus (5th century BC)

Democritus (460-357 BC)

Diagoras of Melos (440-? BC)

Diodorus Cronus (4th century BC)

Diogenes of Sinope (412-323 BC)

Diogenes of Apollonia (460-? BC)

Empedocles (490-430 BC)

Epicurus (341-270 BC)

Eubulides (4th century BC)

Euclides of Megara (450-380 BC)

Eudemus of Rhodes (370-300 BC)

Euhemerus (330-260 BC)

Gorgias (483-378 BC)

Hecataeus (550-476 BC)

Heraclitus (542-480 BC)

Hermarchus (3rd century BC)

Herodotus (490-425 BC)

Hippias (5th century BC)

Leucippus (470-? BC)

Melissus of Samos (482-? BC)

Menippus (3rd century BC)

Parmenides (515-450 BC)

Pherecydes of Syros (580-? BC)

Philolaus (470-385 BC)

Plato (427-347 BC)

Prodicus (460-395 BC)

Protagoras (481-411 BC)

Pyrrho (365-275 BC)

Pythagoras (582-500 BC)

Socrates (469/470-399 BC)

Speusippus (407-339 BC)

Stilpo (380-300 BC)

Strato of Lampsacus (340-268 BC)

Thales (624-546 BC)

Theagenes (565-? BC)

Theophrastus (370-288 BC)

Thrasymachus (459-400 BC)
Timaeus (5th century BC)
Timon (320-230 BC)
Xenocrates (396-314 BC)
Xenophanes (570-478 BC)
Xenophon (429-355 BC)
Zeno of Citium (333-261 BC)
Zeno of Elea (490-430 BC)

ABOUT THE ILLUSTRATIONS

Greek art is rich with images and sculptures of gods and heroes, and scenes from the myths. Although Greek society also took pride in the intellectual achievements of its philosophers, they were not nearly as popular motifs in the arts. It is understandable. The philosophers were thinking and talking, not involved in anything more dramatic than an occasional dispute with a fellow philosopher. Nor were they cherished for their looks.

I had to spend quite some time finding artistic representations of the philosophers, succeeding with most but not all of them. Usually, they are found in the forms of *herms*, sculptured busts placed on a rectangular stone. These busts were rarely – if ever – made at the time when the portrayed philosopher was still alive, so the likeliness was not that likely. Instead, general assumptions about the philosopher's countenance were used. As busts on the herms, they were always quite old and in most cases richly bearded.

Socrates on a herm, c. 2nd century BC. Tradition has it that he looked like a Satyr, and was rather ugly as well.

Other characteristics followed the tradition about the philosopher in question. In some cases there were more than one tradition, with quite differing styles of portraying a philosopher.

The dating of existing sculptures is uncertain, and additionally complicated since many of them are later copies –

often Roman – of lost Greek originals. Therefore, many books simply exclude any such information about the sculptures that are used as illustrations. When I have found reasonably trustworthy information about the illustrations herein, I have included it.

It should be understood that the pictures of the philosophers say more about how we have liked to see them through the ages, than what they really looked like.

LITERATURE

Aristotle, *Metaphysics*, translated by Hugh Lawson-Tancred, London 1998.

Aristotle, *On the Soul*, translated by J. A. Smith, classics.mit.edu.

Aristotle, *Poetics*, translated by Stephen Halliwell, Loeb, London 1999.

Barnes, Jonathan, *The Presocratic Philosophers*, volume 1-2, London 1979.

Boardman, John, *Greek Art*, London 1996.

Bowra, C. M., *Classical Greece*, New York 1965.

Branigan, Keith & Vickers, Michael, *Hellas: The Civilizations of Ancient Greece*, New York 1980.

Cicero, *De natura deorum*, translated by H. Rackham, Loeb, London 1979.

Collignon, Maxime & Harrison, Jane E., *Manual of Mythology in Relation to Greek Art*, London 1890.

Diodorus of Sicily, *The Library of History*, translated by C. H. Oldfather, Cambridge 1970.

Diogenes Laertius, *Lives of Eminent Philosophers*, translated by R. D. Hicks, volume I, Loeb, London 1942.

Diogenes Laertius, *Lives of Eminent Philosophers*, translated by R. D. Hicks, volume II, Loeb, London 1950.

Edmonds, J. M., *Elegy and Iambus*, Loeb, London 1932.

Eliade, Mircea, *The Quest: History and Meaning in Religion*, Chicago 1969.

Euripides, *Bacchae*, translated by Richard Seaford, Warminster 1996.

Evans-Pritchard, E. E., *Theories of Primitive Religion*, Oxford 1965.

Freeman, Kathleen, *The Pre-Socratic Philosophers*, Oxford 1946.

Freeman, Kathleen, *Ancilla to The Pre-Socratic Philosophers*, Oxford 1952.

Gagarin and Cohen (ed.), *The Cambridge Companion to Ancient Greek Law*, Cambridge 2005.

Griaule, Marcel, *Conversations with Ogotemmêli: an Introduction to Dogon Religious Ideas* (Dieu d'eau: entretiens avec Ogotemmêli, 1948), London 1965.

Herodotus, *History*, translated by A. D. Godley, Loeb, London 1981.

Hesiod, *Theogony and Works and Days*, translated by M. L. West, Oxford 1988.

Hinks, R. P., *Greek and Roman Portrait Sculpture*, London 1976.

Homer, *The Iliad*, translation by W. Leaf, 1891, Gutenberg.

Huffman, Carl, Philolaus, *Stanford Encyclopedia of Philosophy*, plato.stanford.edu

Janko, Richard, *Homer, Hesiod and the Hymns: Diachronic Development in Epic Diction*, Cambridge 1982.

Kahn, Charles H., *Anaximander and the Origins of Greek Cosmology*, New York 1960.

O'Connor, Eugene, *The Essential Epicurus*, New York 1993.

Pausanias, *Description of Greece*, Laconia, translated by W.H.S. Jones and H.A. Ormerod, London 1918.

O'Connor, Eugene, *The Essential Epicurus*, New York 1993.

Ong, Walter J., *Orality and Literacy. Technologizing of the Word*, London 1982.

Plato, *Cratylus*, translasted by B. Jowett, 1892, Gutenberg.

Plato, *Cratylus*, translated by Harold N. Fowler, 1921, Perseus.

Plato, *Gorgias*, translated by W. R. M. Lamb, 1967, Perseus.

Plato, *Phaedrus*, translated by Harold N. Fowler, 1925, Perseus.

Plato, *Republic*, translated by Paul Shorey, 1969, Perseus.

Plato, *Theaetetus*.

Plato, *Timaeus*, translated by W. R. M. Lamb, 1925, Perseus.

Plato, *Protagoras*.

Rankin, H.D., *Antisthenes Sokratikos*, Amsterdam 1986.

Riggsby, Andrew M., *Roman Life Expectancy*, utexas.edu/depts/classics/documents/Life.html

Robinson, T. M., *Heraclitus: Fragments*, Toronto 1987.

Sandys, John, *The Odes of Pindar*, Cambridge, Massachusetts 1946.

Schibli, Hermann S., *Pherekydes of Syros*, Oxford 1990.

Sider, David, The Fragments of Anaxagoras, *Beiträge zur Klassischen Philologie* 118, Hain 1981.

Strong, Donald E., *Landmarks of the World's Art: The Classical World*, London 1976.

Tarán, Leonardo, *Parmenides: A Text with Translation, Commentary, and Critical Essays*, Princeton 1965.

Taylor, A. E., *Aristotle on his Predecessors: Being the First Book of his Metaphysics*, Chicago 1910.

Veyne, Paul, *Did the Greeks Believe in their Myths? An Essay on the Constitutive Imagination*, translated by Paula Wissing, Chicago 1988 (the French original was published in 1983).

Villas Boas, Orlando & Claudio, *Xingu: the Indians, their Myths* (original 1970), translated by Susana Hertelendy Rudge, London 1974.

Walker, Susan, *Greek and Roman Portraits*, London 1995.

Wilbur, J. B. & Allen, H. J. (ed.), *The Worlds of the Early Greek Philosophers*, Buffalo 1979.

Wright, M. R., *Empedocles: the Extant Fragments*, New Haven 1981.

Xenophon, *The Apology*, translated by Henry Graham Dakyns, Project Gutenberg.

Xenophon, *Memorabilia*, translated by O. J. Todd, Loeb, London 1979.

www.ingramcontent.com/pod-product-compliance
Lightning Source LLC
Chambersburg PA
CBHW030253130626
46549CB00002B/504